PARENTING

—— *Toward* ——

SOLUTIONS

PARENTING

Toward

SOLUTIONS

HOW TO RAISE

RESPONSIBLE,

LOVING KIDS

Linda Metcalf, Ph.D.

BARNES
&NOBLE
BOOKS
NEW YORK

Dedication

This book is dedicated to our wonderful children,
Roger Jr., Kelli and Ryan,
and to my husband, Roger, whose never-ending
support always gives me the courage to succeed.

This book is also dedicated to my Dad, who always
encouraged me to be creative,
to my Mom who taught me how to love and care.

In memory of Roger's Mom and Dad.

To parents and children everywhere, may you
all receive the respect and love you deserve
from each other. This one's for you!

Acknowledgment

My desire to write a practical, specific, yet *different* parenting book began years ago when I first began talking to parents in a dramatically new way. Thank you, to every person, family, and couple I have had the privilege of knowing and consulting with in private practice. You have made the evolution of these ideas possible on every page of this book! In addition, the ideas presented in this book were enhanced from learning and knowing many admirable colleagues; William O'Hanlon, whose encouragement helped me to believe that my work could be helpful, Brian Cade, whose insight on adolescence and schools has always inspired me, Michael White and David Epston, whose creative work continues to influence how I think. As the model of solution-focused brief therapy continues to evolve, so will your great minds.

Thanks to Connie Kallback and Win Huppuch, who listened to my ideas and said "yes" to my dream. Not only have you given me the gift of two published books, but you have given me friendships I will always treasure, and my first trip to New York City! You made writing this book fun and exciting. Everyone should have four month deadlines!

Thanks to my son, Ryan, 12, for his creativity in producing illustrations that bring my ideas to life. To my oldest son, Roger Jr., 16, whose suggestions on graphics I appreciate and for his design of the *genogram* in chapter one. To Kelli, 14, my daughter and consultant, who is quick to tell me how to create an *environment* in which kids feel comfortable. To my husband, Roger, who always encouraged me to do what I love, you make it possible with your daily support and constant reminders that I can. To my dog, Rolex, who snored along side me for many days and nights, I appreciate your supervision.

To Tami Wiar, my office manager and dear friend, thanks for proofreading the first draft and for giving me a helpful evaluation of the first draft. To Celeste Fender who watched me become too frantic between too many schedules, yet still remained encouraging, thank you for sharing your own parenting "success story." To Chip Chilton, thanks for the telephone brainstorming sessions that helped to develop creative activities that demonstrated what I wanted to say. Thanks finally, to Brian Cade, Larry Furmanczyk, Karen Rayter, and Mike Bishop for sharing with the world, your cases of successful parenting stories. You are making a difference and I am proud to know you.

Finally, thanks to Dr. Scott Miller, Eve Lipchick, Judge Roy Kurban, and Dr. Steven Covey for taking their valuable time to review and comment on this book. I am deeply appreciative and honored to have shared this experience with you.

Foreword

Some time ago, my colleagues and I conducted a little experiment. We showed a videotape of a family we had interviewed to a group of therapists who had come to our center for training. Following the videotape, we asked the therapists to use their skills to describe what they had observed. They very quickly began describing the family and its various members. The mother, the therapists agreed, was obviously an "angry and controlling woman" who was frustrated with her marriage and overwhelmed by her child-rearing responsibilities. Several group members pointed out, however, that the woman's outward expression of anger was really the superficial manifestation of an underlying depression. On the other hand, her husband and the father of their three children was "cut-off and distant" from the family. A few therapists with backgrounds in drug and alcohol counseling identified the signs of a "hidden" drinking problem in the father. Still others identified problems in the eight-year-old daughter. When asked for recommendations, nearly all of the therapists agreed that the family should continue with some sort of family therapy. In addition, they recommended that the mother should be referred to a psychiatrist, the father to an addictions specialist, and the daughter to her own individual therapist.

Once the therapists were finished with their descriptions and recommendations, we informed them that watching the videotape had actually been part of an experiment designed to teach therapists about how their beliefs affect their clinical observations. In reality, the videotape they had all seen was not an actual therapy session and the mother, father, and daughter were not real clients. Moreover, far from being sick, the individuals on the tape were actually part of a healthy, well-functioning family who were discussing and planning an upcoming family picnic! Each time we conducted the experiment, the results were largely the same. At no time did any of the therapists discover our ruse. More troubling, however, is that so few therapists noticed any signs of mental health in this obviously healthy, well-functioning family. How could this be?

Therapists, our study points out, have been trained to find problems. They are, in other words, problem-focused and adept at finding "sickness" as opposed to health, deficits as opposed to capabilities, and weakness as opposed to strengths. As talk radio psychologist Joy Brown recently (and proudly) let on to one of her callers, "You want to know what therapists are good at? They're good at telling people what's wrong with them, that's what they're good at." Of course, there is a kind of common sense appeal to focusing on problems. After all, the reasoning usually goes, people don't seek out a therapist when they are doing well.

What is curious about the tendency to focus on problems and pathology, however, is that forty years of sophisticated research has consistently shown that the factors that have the greatest influence on someone changing is not their problems per se but rather their strengths and resources. Indeed, as counterintuitive as it may sound at first, this same research is showing that what causes and maintains problems is frequently unrelated to what causes and maintains change.

Over the last decade, a pioneering group of practitioners and researchers has taken this research on change and client strengths to heart and made solutions the focus of their work. Rather than studying problems, these solution-focused mental health professionals have been investigating how people rally their own strengths, resources, and abilities to change naturally, spontaneously and on an everyday basis. Until recently, the methods and findings of this new breed of therapists has mostly been confined to professional workshops and publications. Thanks to Dr. Linda Metcalf, the information is finally getting out to the public.

In a step-by-step and clear fashion, Dr. Metcalf outlines the positive, solution-focused techniques that parents can use to help them tap into their own skills and resources for raising healthy, responsible, and loving kids. Her strength lies in providing parents with explicit and simple-to-use exercises for putting the insights on this new therapeutic approach into practice in their daily family life.

You, as parents and caretakers, will have much more than a "good feeling" by the time you finish reading this book—you will have results! I highly recommend it!

Scott D. Miller, Ph.D.
Director, Brief Therapy Training Consortium
Chicago, Illinois

SCOTT D. MILLER, PH.D. is author/co-author of *The Handbook of Solution-Focused Brief Therapy; The Miracle Method: A Radical New Approach to Problem Drinking; Escape from Babel: Toward a Unifying Language for Psychotherapy Practice; Psychotherapy with Impossible Cases.*

About the Author

Linda Metcalf Ph.D., a licensed marriage and family therapist, is a former junior high school teacher, elementary school counselor, and currently a lecturer at the University of Texas at Arlington and Texas Christian University in the Departments of Education. She is the author of several articles on solution-focused brief therapy with children and adolescents, and presents internationally at professional conferences and in-services for teachers, counselors, and parents. She is also the author of *Counseling Toward Solutions: A Practical Solution-Focused Program for Working with Students, Teachers, and Parents* (The Center for Applied Research in Education, 1995).

Dr. Metcalf is in private practice in Arlington, Texas, where she works with children, adolescents, and their families, and consults with school systems as a trainer in solution-focused brief therapy.

Dear Parents,

Kids have changed. Raising our children today as our parents raised us is becoming more and more difficult. Two decades ago, we discouraged kids to speak their mind and give us their opinions. Kids were to be "seen and not heard." Now, decades have passed and our kids are encouraged to express themselves and tell us what they want us to do differently. For many kids, it has been an exhilarating freedom to develop this way; however, without good relationships and communication in their families, this new freedom can also backfire on them, leaving them stranded with out-of-control behaviors. Parenting methods that worked ten or twenty years ago are becoming extinct as our kids evolve.

This book is designed to get your children and adolescents to fall in love with being a part of your family again. If you have tried all of the other approaches to reach your troubled adolescent, stop your child's temper tantrums and anger outbursts, this book is for you. If you are frustrated and are ready to give up on your adolescent because of gang involvement, rebelliousness, drug abuse and a disrespectful attitude, this book is for you. If your child struggles with school problems that only focus on his/her deficits, this book will give you a dramatically new approach to reach his/her teachers! If you are a single parent who feels overwhelmed with home yet are competent at work, this book will give you hope and insight. If you are a stepparent who cannot seem to reach the angry stepchild whom you want as part of your life, this book will help you reach that child. If you are parents of healthy, happy kids and want to keep their spirit alive and your relationship intimate, this book will further your competencies. As a parent in the 2000s, this book will give you a look at your talents and abilities like never before, and guide you into a happy family relationship using the skills you already possess!

Linda Metcalf, Ph.D.
5126 Bridgewater
Arlington, TX 76017

About This Book

Parenting Toward Solutions: How Parents Can Use Skills They Already Have to Raise Responsible, Loving Kids, is written for parents suggesting new ways of rearing and encouraging responsible, competent and self-confident children and adolescents. The parenting ideas included here were developed from the theories of *solution-focused brief therapy* (SFBT), a model of counseling that focuses on the times when a specific problem does *not* occur instead of *why* it happens. Many other problem-solving techniques tend to focus on the cause of certain situations, offering possible explanations for behaviors and then describing strategies to use to solve the problem. The problem with that approach is that the strategies do not work every time with every child or adolescent, leaving the parent frustrated and wondering why their child refuses to change.

The ideas in this book stress a new approach: discovering within parents *themselves* the abilities they already possess that can make changes in the relationship with their children and adolescents. Instead of giving direct instruction for problems, the ideas draw from individual and/or professional competencies parents often develop from job situations, professional talents, and outside friendships or situations. The book invites parents to discover personally, when they have solved other similar problems, and helps them apply their solutions to the situation of concern. Examples help parents apply such *outside* experiences to relationship building, communication struggles, decision making, delegating/follow-up, time management, crises, family losses, anger control, and countless other *common* parenting struggles. While the *situations* may be different, the *skills* developed outside the parenting arena are often the *same* for application at home.

Additionally, parents will find age-specific suggestions for preschoolers who have a fear of the dark, school-aged children who struggle with taunting peers, and rebellious adolescents who require an approach that reduces resistance and encourages cooperation and conversation. Crisis-intervention strategies are suggested for parents to use in traumatic situations such as death and loss of loved ones, gang involvement, drug abuse, and the loss of self-respect. Among other discussed issues are ideas for understanding and talking about suicidal thoughts, AIDS and sex, depression, anger, and other common and important issues among children and adolescents. Dramatically new ways of approaching school problems that assist educators in thinking and observing kids differently are included in a step-by-step format. Additionally, the transition into college and adulthood for both parent and child *and* parent and grandparent are discussed as a new way of "relating and seeing" each other. The book ends with stories from therapists and families from around the world describing "exceptional" parenting and solution-seeking behaviors.

Throughout the book, case studies demonstrate new ways of seeking solutions so that the ideas discussed make sense to parents and are easy to apply immediately. Many chapters have worksheets, exercises, and activities for families, couples, individuals and specific situations. Each chapter begins with a case study to illustrate the content, approach, and strategy of the subject matter and contains easy-to-follow dialogue from the cases to show new ways of talking and working with children and adolescents.

Chapter 1 invites you to begin looking at your current talents, competencies and successes professionally, socially, as a co-worker and parent. The chapter includes reproducible sheets for a significant other, parent, co-workers, and children to complete that solicit talents, abilities, and situations which were handled competently and received well in the past. This new source of information takes you to a new perception as you learn how your family, co-workers, and friends perceive various skills you have in other situations. This new transition from other successful situations outside or inside the home generates more productive interacting at home. The solutions you discover are more likely to be used with your spouse and children since they have already been successful elsewhere.

Chapter 2 is designed to assist you with realistic and achievable goal setting. Goals are difficult to set when a problem seems "bigger than life" in the family. The chapter begins with a case study illustrating how *redescribing* a situation can change the focus and lead to an achievable goal. Thereafter, ten philosophical "assumptions" are suggested for *redescribing* parenting problems so that you begin to think differently about the problem at hand. Thinking differently leads to interacting and behaving differently for parents and kids. The ideas in this chapter discourage blaming others, confrontation, and labeling; instead, it suggests ideas for you to use that assist kids to solve their own problems. Instead of lecturing kids on "the right way," this chapter encourages a major shift in the *relationship* with parents and kids.

Chapter 3 describes the typical attributes of adolescents and suggests new conversational strategies to get their attention and make change more probable. Conversational strategies and new ways of *thinking* about your adolescent will allow a different interaction and, therefore, different result.

A research study is included in this chapter that is composed of direct quotations from teenagers, ages 13 to 16. The remarks made by the teens on a wide variety of subjects serve as an informative way of relaying to parents everywhere what *works* with adolescents. Additionally, ideas for discussing AIDS and sex with your adolescent are specifically addressed.

Chapter 4 suggests an additional way to look at problems—externalizing them for attack! This chapter also explores different ways that families maintain problems through each individual's actions, and how they can conquer the problem through new behaviors. Several case studies are discussed in detail, showing examples of how families can work with anxious children. Additionally, a discussion of labels—such as ADD or ADHD, major depression, anger disorders, attitudes, and temper tantrums—includes suggestions for seeking help, talking to teachers, or adjusting lifestyles to lessen the influence of these descriptions on individuals.

Chapter 5 touches on serious problems and allows you for the first time to assess your children's *symptoms* and then look for *exceptions* to those symptoms, leading to solutions and lessening worry. Such serious situations as suicide, depression, anger, and ADHD are discussed with clinical information and then enhanced with information from "exceptions." Within the "exceptions" lie clues for you to identify and use to lessen the symptoms and assist your children. The situations are explained thoroughly, using case studies to clarify, and reveal successful strategies of exceptional parents that conquered the label's impact on their child or adolescent. You will find this chapter reassuring and informative.

Chapter 6 encompasses school problems and how to solve them from kindergarten through twelfth grade. It supplies dramatically different strategies for working out conflicts with teachers and children so that everyone benefits. Specific steps, ideas, and strategies for calling, scheduling, and holding a *solution-focused* parent/teacher conference are given, complete with a form to take to the meeting. You will find additional suggestions for talking to teachers in a new way, thereby gaining the teacher's assistance in identifying when school *works*. The chapter also stresses the importance of parental involvement in school issues and supplies case studies describing typical school issues with successful endings.

Chapter 7 deals specifically with strategies for helping children and adolescents through a crisis situation that may deal with death, loss, gang involvement, sexual activity, and drug abuse. The suggestions for dissolving the impact of these problems are reinforced by several case studies that describe children and adolescents on the brink of crisis and helpful methods that brought them resolution and comfort. Sheets to duplicate and conversation guides that help you talk with your children and adolescents are provided as a support as well as a resource.

Chapter 8 deals with the young adult's "flight" from the family and transitions that fall on parent and child. Suggestions for coping are outlined in this chapter so that you have a guide by which to respond and "let go" at appropriate times. This difficult time is made easier by *redescribing* and *reminiscing past successes* of the child and parent. Accountability of children through their past successes, abilities, and accomplishments serves as a comfort to you as you "launch" your children into the world. Couples who relinquish parenting responsibilities in trade for newfound freedom will find suggestions that enable them to reenter their time together and enjoy their future years in couplehood once again.

The Appendix describes many cases of exceptional families from *around the world!* The families are presented and described through the use of rich dialogues that promise to give hope, practical ideas, and examples to even the most desperate parents. These case studies reinforce the ideas in the chapters of the book and support the strategies described. The Appendix will also give methods of working with kids from a therapist's point of view, so that you may enter a new arena and begin to see how solution-focused interventions are formulated.

Contents

Chapter 6
School Problems: You **Can** Influence the Outcome   **141**

Chapter 7
Talking to Kids During Times of Crisis   **171**

Chapter 8
Preparing for the Launch   195

Appendix:
Stories of Exceptional Families from Around the World   207

References   235

Index   239

Chapter
1

Mining Your Own Resources

An Introduction to Parenting Toward Solutions

The reasonable man adapts himself to the world:
the unreasonable one persists in trying to adapt the world to himself.
Therefore all progress depends on the unreasonable man."

—George Bernard Shaw

A recently divorced and exhausted mother confided to me once that she could not get her kids under control since she and her husband had divorced. He had been the disciplinarian and had often undermined her authority. Through our short conversation I learned she was a fifth-grade teacher who had always received excellent evaluations. I asked her how she had achieved such success in the classroom for over ten years and she described her strategies: "I post the rules in the classroom, follow-through with consequences, praise often, listen to kids' complaints and try to be fair, stay calm and compliment them whenever I can." When I suggested that she try using the strategies that worked with the children at school with her own children at home, at first she questioned the idea, but then she agreed to try them as an experiment. These "new parenting strategies" were at first uncomfortable to think about but after recognizing her obvious success at school, she settled with the possibility that they might work. Still hesitant, she questioned the possibility that home and work were very different relationships. I agreed with her and then said, "Yes, but the skills might be the same. . . . Let's see what happens. . . . You have certainly developed some successful ideas."

Within one week, she had her kids' attention and her self respect blossomed. She was successful in her strategies because the strategies were uniquely hers, giving her confidence to try something new at home. Since the strategies were used in another context, experimenting with them at home was more comfortable. I reminded her, upon ending our first conversation, to remember that it may take time for her own kids to "catch on," similarly to how it takes time for her new classes to catch on to new school rules. After two weeks she reported that her kids had initially rebelled against the new rules but that she stuck to them as she would have in the classroom and they adapted well.

Changing Your Focus Can Help to Dissolve the Problem!

What is different and unique about this approach to parenting? Could finding solutions to family problems be so simple? Yes. When people search for the reasons *why* problems occur, they discover many reasons for their problems. The result? *Possible* explanations but no new strategies. If the mother in the previous case had searched hard enough, she might have come up with all sorts of reasons why her children were not behaving and even worse, given them excuses for their unruly, disrespectful behavior towards her.

Initially, the mother saw herself as incompetent and her ex-husband as competent and was concerned that she could not fill the role as her husband had. She was unable to see her successes outside of her home because she had separated her various responsibilities and abilities into different categories instead of applying them into *many* categories. Like many of us, she saw her home life as an entity in itself, which required special talents applicable to only that situation. She had lost sight of her abilities in other areas when her life had changed, forgetting to *mine her own resources* as a successful teacher. As she began to search for answers from an area in which she was already successful and stopped looking for *why* she and her children were not getting along, she came up with the following discoveries:

1. **"I'm successful in getting kids to listen to me in the classroom."**

   In her professional life, she was able to create a classroom in which kids listened, followed rules, and respected her. She did this through consistency, posting rules, complimenting and respecting the students, listening to their worries, and being kind, fair and flexible.

2. **"I need to change the way I am thinking about my children."**

   She changed her own perception of her children. Instead of seeing them as defiant, impossible and difficult, she looked at them as children in transition, similar to her students at the beginning of each new school year. By looking at them this way, she lessened her defensiveness and went to work to create an environment at home similar to that at school.

3. **"If I can manage classroom behavior well, maybe I can manage my children's behavior."**

   Instead of seeing herself as incompetent and her ex-husband as competent, she now saw herself as full of many skills she had forgotten to use. This discovery in itself gave her the confidence to begin creating a new environment at home with her own children, and gave her the determination to follow through.

Why the Best Resources Are Your Own!

In my experience as a family therapist, my clients have taught *me* the best techniques for dealing with their children and adolescents. Rarely, using a problem-focused approach, have I been able to prescribe parenting techniques and strategies that gave *all* families success. They were too different in lifestyle, ethnicity, and culture! It simply was not fair to imply that the standard parenting strategies were a *cure* for everyone and usually, the strategies I suggested as *traditional* had already been tried ... with failure. Additionally, counseling from other therapists, parenting classes, and seminars were all that parents thought were available as resources. The parents obviously saw the outside help as the only resources and failed to look within themselves for answers. When these outside avenues failed, chants of *"we may have to send him to military school," "we may need to put her in a psychiatric hospital,"* and *"I don't care anymore, I give up!"* were common, regrettable decisions and statements that parents made out of frustration. Unfortunately, their best efforts to change their offspring did not involve changing *their* parenting styles, and revolved around other *prescribed strategies* that did not fit their particular offspring. As their parenting style remained the same, the problems usually resurfaced or refused to be resolved.

How, then is it possible that members of the family *themselves* can discover the very best solutions? For one thing, no one knows their families better than the members themselves. I once talked with an extremely volatile family, whose members desired to curtail their violence and renew their relationships. I asked them to describe any time when they could discuss a subject without fighting and hurting each other. One of the daughters, age 10, looked up and said, "That's easy, when we're in public. I guess we're afraid people will stare at us so we keep it down." A wise discovery for the family. Just the recognition that they were capable of discussing an issue without physically hurting each other was surprising to them. It also led them to explore other times and places when and where violence did not occur. The problems encountered by other families often contain similar themes, yet rarely do the strategies they develop to overcome the problems using this approach turn out similarly. This confirms that the strategies need to be as unique as the family members themselves.

Forget Labeling ... Find Your Own Description!

During the past few decades, many techniques have been created and devised to *cure* many different behavioral and emotional problems of children and adolescents. The diagnoses used to explain behaviors have become extensive and unfortunately have given us reasons to consider as to *why* kids act out and behave as they do. Understanding *why* problems occur gives us information but no direction or strategies for solutions. Kids who are labeled often end up with excuses that inhibit them and the significant others in their life from expecting normal, responsible behavior. Even worse, the diagnoses are simply another way of describing behaviors that could be described in many ways. The description can and often does magnify the behavioral concern so that the situation seems hopeless. The diagnoses become *barbed wire fences* which keep us *STUCK*. They give us possible reasons why our children and adolescents *can't* function as we wish they would. This curbs our attempts to use our own instincts at times in a productive manner, after thorough observation.

Additionally, in spite of diagnoses, or knowing "why" their kids act as they do, parents *continue* to be frustrated and kids continue to act out. Timeouts stop working, grounding becomes ineffective, kids run away or become rebellious and defiant, and worst of all, parents sometimes give up. Speaking as a parent of three adolescents, I can assure everyone who reads this book that by using these ideas, you, your child or adolescent will have a new opportunity to explore and identify possible strategies that may make a difference in your relationship. Your job as a parent is to provide an environment in which your child or adolescent can feel good about himself or herself and discover these new strategies *with* you.

Creating the Opportunity for Change

Parenting Toward Solutions means that parents understand how seeing and approaching situations differently allow children and adolescents the opportunity to solve their own problems *and*, by doing so, lessens dependence and encourages responsibility. It means that parents assist their kids with identification of the *exceptions,* or, the times when the problem is not occurring, stimulating a new view of the problem and—more important—how it is maintained between parent and child. Instead of focusing on the fact that the child is having a problem, the new focus becomes one of figuring out who is doing what when the problem is absent. Then, utilizing current skills and the identified exceptions, the parents begin to think differently about the problem, act differently with their children, and the children act differently toward the parents. Observe the following case in which a Mom visualizes her daughter differently, interacts very differently, and produces a more pleasant result.

Angie

Mom and Angie, age 13, typically have conflict when Angie refuses to clean her room. After some self-examination, Mom realizes that the times when her daughter listens to her are when Mom is:

a. calm and not yelling

b. really intrigued and interested in what Angie is doing

c. offers a reward or privilege in response to a task that needs to be done

d. allows Angie sufficient time to complete a task

With this information in mind and a determination just for today to *not* let a problem grow between her and her daughter, on Saturday morning at 11:00, Mom walks calmly into Angie's room. Mom smiles, touches her fondly, and asks Angie what she has planned for the day. Angie, preoccupied with finding just the right outfit for the mall, sighs, looks at Mom momentarily, surprised that Mom seems genuinely interested and says, "Why?" Mom typically comes in on Saturdays with a frustrated look after observing Angie's very messy room. Angie *tells* Mom that she is going to meet two friends at the mall at 2:00. Instead of being confrontive, Mom replies: "That sounds like fun. Tell you what, I'll be glad to take you when you make your bed, bring the clothes to the hamper, and pick up your dishes. I remember how much fun I had when I used to go to the movies on Saturdays with my friends. Tell you what, I'm going downstairs anyway so I'll help out by taking these dishes with me. I'll be downstairs when you finish picking things up. Let me know when you're finished and we can make some definite plans."

What's *different* about the interaction this time?

- Perhaps the parent is speaking differently to Angie. Instead of being frustrated and demanding, she is "stepping into Angie's world" and realizing how important the mall and her friends are instead of cleaning her room. She thought about when she was an adolescent and realized that friends were definitely more fun than making the bed.

- Perhaps Angie is more aware of how she is responding to her Mom. Instead of yelling this morning, she notices that Mom seems genuinely interested and this gives her little reason to yell back. Angie likes feeling important and accepted by her parents and she likes it when Mom does not yell. After all, if Mom does not yell, Angie has less of a reason to fight back.

- Being thirteen is difficult at times, since Angie is searching for acceptance, validation, and a sense of being important to someone. Usually it's her friends who give her all three of these, but this morning, it's Mom. Mom is not inviting a problem to occur by interacting differently with her daughter. It surprises Angie, who *has* to respond differently as well.

- Perhaps Mom is seeing the problem of Angie's messy room differently, not as a sign of laziness but as a sign that Angie has other important things to do. Mom has decided that, as an experiment for herself, she would not allow a problem to grow between herself and her daughter.

- Mom decides to participate in the activity. By doing this, it decreases the chance of "slavery" as adolescents tend to refer to chores and tasks. It also, again, communicates that Mom is there for Angie, to assist her in getting what she wants as well. This does not mean that Mom will do the entire job, it simply means that her slight participation in cleaning with Angie communicates that Mom is on her side.

Chances are that Angie will possibly begin to see her Mom as liking her more, something not only vital to adolescents, but appealing as well. Teens tend to act out when they feel unaccepted and criticized. Their obvious lack of social skills (due to their small amount of time on earth) in expressing their hurt effectively leads them instead to stomp out of the room, slam the door, screech the tires, break dishes, and fail school. Their attempt to *show* their parents that they cannot hurt them as they do is frivolous and ineffective, usually ending in more confrontation. Instead, Mom realized these traits of her teenage daughter and *cooperated* with her daughter's needs. The result? Less resistance and more of an opportunity to create an atmosphere where both Mom and Angie could get what they both wanted, harmoniously.

Unique Kids Deserve Unique Strategies

For years, parents have often looked to the *experts* for guidance and have applied suggestions that sometimes have worked. Most of the time techniques such as behavior modification work . . . on those kids who rarely misbehave or act out. But what about the children and adolescents with whom these ideas *don't work?* These interventions are most often done *to* kids, resulting in a parent's continuous need to constantly, consistently remind them to do things differently. Angie's Mom had tried them all. She became frustrated and then guilt-ridden for not being able to reach her daughter. Rewards and consequences had worked for her older daughter, but Angie responded rebelliously to those strategies.

Strict, structured interventions work for kids who are receptive to parental authority. They realize they are in error and they listen to their parents' concerns. However, what happens to the other group of offspring who are not quite so receptive to staying on track? When situations arise and a parent is not present, kids feel lost and have a difficult time relying on themselves. Instead, they get off track, in trouble and their parents need to redirect them . . . constantly. Strict, punitive parent-centered techniques do not encourage growth; rather, they encourage dependence and, often, rebellion. Today's kids are offered too many opportunities for deviance and are encouraged by their peers, media, and music to rebel. For these youngsters, the approach to *reach* them must be as unique as they are. The key

 to finding these unique approaches is to reflect on past strategies that worked, even if years ago. While your acting-out teenager may be taller than you, inside she is the same child you raised years ago. Recall what worked then and you will have a starting place for today.

How Recalling the Past Can Offer Solutions for the Future!

Suppose in the near future when your child or adolescent acts up, has a problem with a peer, fails at a task or subject at school, instead of prodding for why the situation occurred and saying, "I told you not to do that" or "how could you let this happen," you might ask *instead:*

1. *"I'll bet you would like things to be much different than they are now. Tell me, how would you like things to be when they are better soon?"*

2. *"Tell me, how did you solve the problem with Susie last time?"*

3. *"I remember that you passed your spelling test two weeks ago. . . . Do you remember when you did that? What do you remember you/us doing that helped you?"*

4. *"What do you think it will take to get un-grounded? I remember a time when you calmed down and cleaned your room and I let you out early. What do you think?"*

5. *"What do you think your teacher might need to see so that I don't get any more calls this week? What do you think she would say if you asked her?"*

6. *"What can I do so that lying to me is not necessary? When was the last time you felt comfortable telling me something important/personal? What was I doing that made it possible for you to feel okay about it?"*

How are these questions *different* from those you have asked before? They do not address *why* the problem occurred; instead, they immediately ask the child/adolescent for strategies, or, what you could do as their parent to help. The questions do not blame or accuse, criticize or condemn. Those strategies are unproductive and will invite the problem to become monstrous between you. Even if your child/adolescent replies that he wants the teachers off his back, for you to un-ground him, or to get the bully at school to lay off, agree with him. Remember, children/adolescents' goals are often very different from ours. We may want our kids to resolve differences with their teachers so that they will learn how to work with others and take responsibility for their actions. The adolescent, on the other hand, may just want to work things out so that he will be able to go to the dance on Friday. Their reason should be respected, for they are more likely to work towards their goal than ours. Your agreement that their goal is worthwhile will:

a. lower resistance

b. raise confidence in your kids

c. motivate them to change

Even if your child or adolescent may not seem to deserve your total respect *yet,* give him or her some respect for just being your child. If this sounds absurd, remember, you are not declaring war . . . you are building a relationship. You would probably not build a friendship with defensiveness and cruel remarks. The true motivator for future success occurs when they experience *some* current successes. Assist them with keeping their goals reasonable, specific, and obtainable over a very *short period of time*. For example:

- encourage your first grader to work on sharing for only one afternoon
- help your fifth grader to watch how he avoids fighting for a day at a time
- your high school junior might want to watch how she avoids talking back for two or three days
- your live-in college student might find some ways in which he can work part time during the school year to earn the money he seldom has, just by observing himself for a week during classes

The reasons for such short-term goals? They are achievable. A little success will go a long way toward attempts at future success.

The Job of Raising Loving, Respectful, and Responsible Kids

As parents, we are in the business of producing competent, productive, self-loving, and responsible adults. It has been my experience that the approach described in this book encourages such responsibility and at the same time lessens resistance as children and adolescents see parents as allies instead of enemies. Many families who are currently using this approach testify that their lives have become less complicated and that they enjoy their children and adolescents more, since they *see* themselves and their offspring differently. Instead of seeing kids as problem-ridden, their parents see them as *bothered* by problems, and their job as one of creating an environment in which the problems do not take over. In the process of creating that environment, the discoveries you make personally will offer you the solutions you have been searching for.

"In the beginner's mind there are many possibilities;
in the expert's mind there are few."

—Zen, Suzuki, 1970

Look at Yourself Through a New Lens

Consider a real possibility: you *already* have the capability to be a more effective parent and your kids already have the capacity to be responsible, caring, and problem-solving kids. The first step to *parenting towards solutions* is to look within yourself, identifying and learning about how your present skills can change into more effective parenting skills. Chances are that you are already successful somewhere—in your professional life, social life, outside leisure activities, or home life. Your kids may already be star soccer players, honor students, artists, or even kids who make friends easily, even if they are not the friends you would choose. Even if your child/adolescent is troubled at school, there may be days when he or she is not in detention and makes a passing grade. These are the "exceptions" I encourage you to begin to notice and verbalize. They are the beginnings of seeing your-

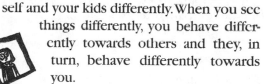

self and your kids differently. When you see things differently, you behave differently towards others and they, in turn, behave differently towards you.

At work, you get feedback on how you are progressing through raises or promotions when you succeed. At home, things just keep on going the way they did with no increase in rank and little information about what you do well. The following exercises are designed to help you self-discover what works for you in other areas of your life and help you to apply them at home with those you love, successfully. They are also designed so that your significant family members can give you input and insight about your abilities. This new interaction in itself will begin to change in your family life. After working with adolescents for fifteen years I've discovered that a common desire of young people is to be asked what their ideas and opinions are. By asking questions, you may discover a wealth of information even in a rebellious adolescent, especially if you act sincere and curious about his or her opinion. Even your preschooler or school-age child will be able to describe happy times with you, since his or her thinking is so concrete. Your spouse/partner who knows you best may be able to recall your early days together and remember what was attractive about you. Your family's feedback will help you to develop your solutions and, when you listen to what they say specifically, you can't miss.

Learning to Recognize What Works

For a moment, recall last week and make a list of what *did not work out* at home or the office? Write them below:

1. _____

2. _____

3. _____

4. _____

5. _____

How many situations were on the first list? Most of us can recall those times rather efficiently and quickly. Tough, unhappy situations stand out in our minds because they cause us to act differently, changing and rearranging our plans. Now, look back at last week and notice *what worked* at home or the office. Write these below:

1. _____

2. _____

3. _____

4. _____

5. _____

If you found that the second list was more difficult, you are in the majority. These times are more difficult to recognize since they often make the day flow quickly and do not make problems for us. This makes them very difficult to identify. However, were there any "exceptions" or strategies in the second list that made things pleasant or not *so difficult?* If not, look closer. When were things at their worst on the first list? Now, when were they *slightly tolerable or better than the worst? Did these instances make it to your second list?* How did you manage to get back on track?

During those times, if we looked through the lens of a video camera, we could see what you or your family members/office workers did that made a difference. Sure, other people often have a hand in those good days (the boss who gave you a pat on the back) and we should give them credit. However, let's not doubt for a second that those close to us aren't influenced by us. The next and most important question to consider is, "How did I influence those people to act the way they did toward me?" How did you get your boss to realize you deserved his approval? Realize you had a hand in creating that situation?

If you took a poll of your acquaintances, friends, relatives, co-workers, bosses, trainees, spouse and children, they could probably identify some of your assets. How do *you* think they would describe you if a reporter interviewed them? What would they list as your qualities? These are budding parenting skills! The fact that you have picked up this book to read tells me that you can be a competent parent who desires more from your family life. It tells me that it is important to you to reach your children and raise them in an exceptional way. However, you may be stuck in a belief that you have to parent a certain way because maybe your parents are telling you so or because an expert on parenting has told you what to do. All you know is that the strategies that others tell you about don't seem to fit with your own beliefs or abilities in other areas, so you tend to start off using them but do them less and less.

What Are Your Secrets to Working With Others?

Many of us who have employees *learn how to treat the employees* so that we get their maximum efforts. We wouldn't imagine doing something that would slow them down or make them unproductive. We put on our best faces and our best attitudes so that they in turn feel good about their performance. Those of us who are employees tend to respond to our boss so we keep our job, get a raise, etc. Even our best friends require a certain attention and consideration to be in a fulfilling relationship with us. We make this happen by thinking about our actions instead of waiting for *them* to change. The divorced mother described at the beginning of this chapter could have waited for her children to change behaviors, but her frustration level would have increased and her children might not have responded to her so quickly and

 effectively, especially if they sensed she was unsure. She helped her own children to have structure and routine in their lives by first changing herself, then she added nurturing, rewards, and compassion—tools that won her high evaluations and granted her children a feeling of safety.

A Parent Learns About Setting His Own "Limits"

Sometimes, the task of discovering what works with others can be as simple as scheduling in a time to do things differently. For example, in the following example, Stephen, an engineer, considered himself to be organized, scheduled, logical in his decision-making skills, yet understanding towards his supervisees when they were troubled. Unfortunately, he was bringing supervisory skills home with him and forgetting to be there for his family emotionally. After some thought about how he managed himself at the office, he discovered a new way of "supervising his family:"

Stephen's family came to counseling with the intention of trying to tame their husband and father's roaring personality at home. His family complained that he was inconsiderate, boisterous and rude to them, and they often encouraged him to travel instead of coming home at night! After he came alone and described his concern, I began to ask him how his employees would describe him at work. He said they would probably describe him as a kind, assertive, flexible, and understanding boss. He apparently listened before raising his voice (if he did so at all) at work and always considered the past record of the employee before he spoke. From that information, I asked, "If you were to use these strategies this week with your thirteen-year-old son John, how would you deal with him differently?" Pondering over this question, he described radically new strategies. He also decided to "schedule" a new approach when he saw

the city limit sign after his long drive home. He decided that once he saw the sign, he was to remind himself that it was time to be Dad and not the supervisor. This made sense to him. Within two weeks his family life improved.

What did the father learn about himself as he discovered his abilities and transferred them to his home?

1. He could utilize certain skills from work, as noted by his wife and co-workers, with his family so they saw him as his co-workers and supervisees did.

2. He considered what he wanted different at home and approached the goal as if it were the most important "project" he would ever have.

3. He learned that when he changed his approach, his family changed their behaviors.

4. He noticed that starting small led to bigger change. He found it became easier to change himself when he changed his thinking from his family being "defensive and lazy" to "they have a lot to do at home and they must have a lot on their minds . . . I need to give them a break." These were the similar thoughts he often had regarding his employees.

As Stephen discovered, many of us develop skills for *other* relationships that supply our basic needs for living and holding a job. For example, the additional professions below describe possible skills and qualities typical of each position:

Engineer: Thinking is detailed and logical. Good ability to hear specific details and remember the important points of others.

Supervisor: Ability to listen well to others, delegate, and manage people so that they are productive.

Doctor/Dentist: Ability to hear complaints and respond with a suggestion that is helpful, not critical. Ability to assist others in feeling comfortable with themselves and the situation.

Clerical/Secretarial: Ability to organize, manage, prioritize, and still have time to smile and listen.

Attorney: Ability to listen for details, offer possible options, and possibilities/outcomes for certain situations. Good ability to do research on ideas/problems at hand.

Counselor/Teacher: Ability to listen, understand, assist and offer suggestions, continue to try ideas until successful, prompt, and encourage.

Construction Worker: Ability to get a job done on time, plan, organize and complete what is asked of him or her. Active, with a creative ability to think of many ways to accomplish a task.

Musician, Artist, Computer Designer: Creativity in thought and strategy. Sensitive to other's insight and talents ... enjoys individuality and is respectful of it.

Housewife: Multi-talented! Able to perform many tasks productively and efficiently. A "jack of all trades." Able to prioritize and provide a nurturing environment under the stress of childrearing.

Office Manager: Able to perform many tasks under stress and still keep cool under pressure. Able to organize, prioritize, and keep relationships among co-workers pleasant. Knowledgeable about the times to avoid conflict and allow others to work out differences.

...and many more!

Additionally, many of us are good friends, committee members, chairpeople who are successful at our roles. How do we manage these tasks successfully? How do you explain your ability to raise funds, chair a PTA meeting, run a school carnival, find time to volunteer for your favorite charity?

How do you cheer an ill relative or celebrate an accomplishment of a peer? How did you learn these skills to begin with? Do you recall time with your mother, father, aunt or uncle that left you with an impression of how you would like the relationship with your family to be?

This first exercise is designed to help you explore the traits and qualities of your family members. By looking at the environment from which you came, you will have the opportunity to discover the parenting methods you might have experienced. You can now choose to continue with those methods you approve of and omit those that do not fit your current needs or desires for your family. Do not worry if you do not like the parenting you received. You have already created a better family life by seeking information in this book. You can now break a cycle or continue one at your own decision. Also look at aunts and uncles, cousins, and grandparents whom you knew and admired. Seek out the traits you loved and recall how they behaved that made them dear to you.

A Solution-Oriented Genogram
Adapted from Bruce Kuehl, Ph.D. (1995)

A *family genogram* is a symbolic diagram that shows your family members, their traits, relationships, children, and ancestors. "By graphically representing the evolution of a family through time, the solution-oriented genogram becomes an important documentation of change . . . that clients can help construct along the way, adding a sense of personal investment that can increase the document's meaningfulness." (Kuehl, p. 224, 1995)

Page 18 shows a sample of a complete genogram, introducing Mary and Fred, Jr., parents who were interested in improving their parenting skills. From looking at their family history, they initially felt they were not carrying on any negative parenting styles of their parents. They were both motivated, education-minded adults who wanted their children to be motivated, education-minded children and adolescents. However, their attempts at communicating how to do this with each other were keeping them stuck and feeling incompetent. By looking at their genogram, they were able to see how they have *already* adapted some competent parenting styles and helped them to identify even more.

From the sample genogram, it seems that Mary and Fred, Jr. have brought many of their parents' traits to their current family, yet have omitted some. Let's examine how these two people emerged from their *nuclear family.*

Mary

Mary, reared in a hard-working environment in which she was discouraged to speak her opinion or pursue an education, apparently decided—upon having her own children—to talk to them, listen, and be involved with their lives. During Mary's years as a parent, many parenting theories encouraged parents to talk more to their children and become attached to them. Additionally, she pursued an education that affected her own children and their view of a female's role in the family. Mary was an extrovert in her family and was physically abused by her father for expressing her dislike for his poor treatment of her mother. She was careful to choose a husband who would be kind to her and support her ideas with childrearing. When he became critical of her during their early marriage, she quickly informed him that this was not acceptable to her. She took a job and became more independent. Fred, Jr., in turn, stopped the verbal criticism and turned it toward the children. Mary spent much of her time consulting with her husband regarding his verbal criticisms and, eventually, he stopped. She brought her father's stern manner and high expectations to her marriage and to her family.

Fred, Jr.

Fred was reared primarily by a nanny, whom he loved very much. His father was rarely home, being a prominent surgeon in the city. His mother was kind, caring, yet busy doing charity work for various social clubs. He and his sister and brother enjoyed many vacations at their grandparents' homes in addition to each other's company, since his parents were rarely present. When Fred went to college, he dated many girls and chose a woman to marry who was nurturing, caring, and sweet. As he and Mary began having children, Fred spent more time at the office and the golf course, leaving Mary to rear the children. Secretly, Fred felt incompetent about being a parent and knew that Mary was much better at taking care of the children. When he felt badly about his role as a parent, he would often scream at the children and Mary would talk to him about more effective ways to reach them. Fred eventually learned how to parent later in life when the children were teenagers.He brought his father's determination and respect for education to his marriage and to parenting.

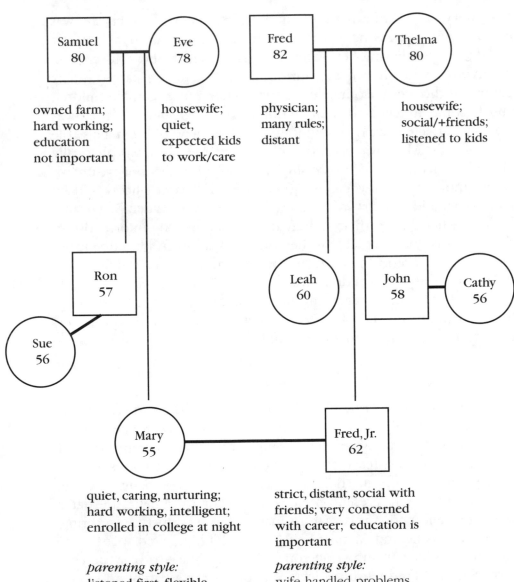

Samuel 80 — **Eve 78**	**Fred 82** — **Thelma 80**
owned farm; hard working; education not important	housewife; quiet, expected kids to work/care
	physician; many rules; distant
	housewife; social/+friends; listened to kids

Ron 57

Sue 56

Leah 60

John 58 — **Cathy 56**

Mary 55 — **Fred, Jr. 62**

quiet, caring, nurturing;
hard working, intelligent;
enrolled in college at night

parenting style:
listened first, flexible,
understanding, involved
with children's school.

strict, distant, social with
friends; very concerned
with career; education is
important

parenting style:
wife handled problems,
supported wife's rules for
kids, little time for children
until teens, verbally abusive
to children

Mary and Fred as Parents

Mary and Fred, Jr. reared three children. All three went to college and married well. Fred III became a physician; Susan, a teacher; and Roger, an accountant. Each child developed healthy relationships with friends.

Like many new families, Mary and Fred learned from each other and stressed the importance of their various family traits. When the traits did not work with their new family, they disregarded them and consulted each other for better ones. When Mary struggled with something Fred did with the children, she recognized that waiting until the conflict was over gave her an opportunity to approach him respectfully, something he needed. When Fred disapproved of Mary, he realized that he had to be verbally respectful to her in order to be listened to. They were successful as parents because they developed unique parenting styles that fit each of them, although each style was different.

Directions for Constructing Your Own Genogram

The next exercise is designed for you to draw your genogram and list, beside each person, traits he or she contributed to your family history. As you write them down, you may be surprised that you have transferred what happened in your family, positive or negative, to your current family. Consider yourself the *new author of* **your** *family.* Now is your opportunity to choose which traits you wish to continue as a family tradition and omit those that do not fit your role as a parent.

If, as you look over your genogram, you realize that the parenting you received was **not** the parenting you wish to give your children, don't despair. While research suggests that the traits of older generations tend to be passed on to the new generation, I believe that when **you** realize how you want your family life to be, you can change your parenting style through this new knowledge. Now is your chance to create a new legacy for your family! Even if your childhood involved abuse, this is your opportunity to *step out of the old story mentally,* break free and escape from the prison of feeling as if you were a victim, creating a new story for your family in the process.

Therefore, feel free to list the parenting skills of others on your genogram, even if **you** now choose to leave them out of your family relationships. Compliment yourself for recognizing the skills you wish to bring to your family. You are now learning to watch for strategies you think will work with your kids and recognizing those that will not work. If your partner is interested in completing her or his own genogram, make sure to copy the exercise so that you can each complete your own.

1. Place the names of your grandmothers in the circles at the top of the page, and your grandfathers' names in the squares at the top of the page. Inside of the circle or square, write their ages. If they are deceased, mark the circle or square with a large "X." If your grandparents divorced, place a slash through the line that connects them. If any grandparent remarried, draw a horizontal line from that parent outside of the diagram and place a new symbol at the end of the line for the new spouse. Continue this process if there are multiple marriages and divorces, using a slash for each divorce.

2. Below your grandparents, draw a vertical line for each of your grandparents' children; your parents, aunts and uncles. Draw circles to represent the females and squares to represent the males. Make your parents' circle or square larger, and draw it slightly lower than the rest of their siblings. (See the example on page 21.) Place the ages and an "X" inside the symbol if any of the siblings are deceased. Do this for each side.

3. Draw a horizontal line between each of your parents to symbolize marriage/living together. Place a slash to indicate a divorce and a new horizontal line toward the outside of the diagram if a parent remarried or entered a new relationship.

4. Draw yourself, your brothers and sisters with vertical lines, circles or squares, ages, etc., between your parents (or stepparents). Look at each person you have listed on your genogram. Below each diagram, write individual traits and parenting strategies, whether positive or negative. Attempt to look for qualities you remember fondly. You may find that looking through an old photo album may be helpful or consulting with your partner about family members.

Genogram

Grandparents

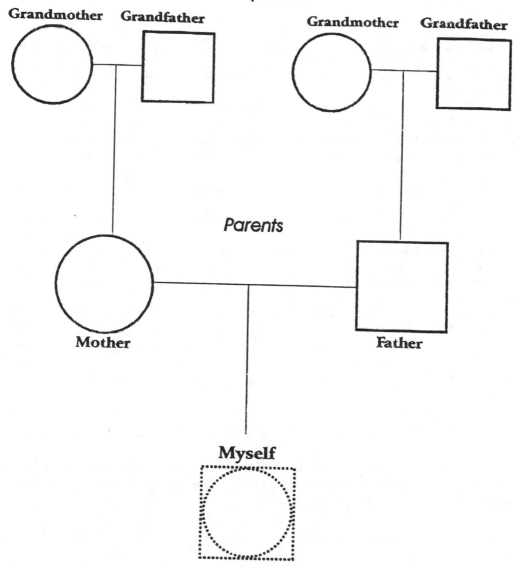

Grandmother **Grandfather** **Grandmother** **Grandfather**

Parents

Mother **Father**

Myself

Genogram Discussion Page

Whose traits, if any, are currently influencing your parenting style?

_____

_____

_____

_____

Which person(s) and parenting traits did you admire the most? What did they teach you about parenting, as you look back at your time with them?

_____

_____

_____

_____

Which person(s)' parenting traits would you like to eliminate from your family?

_____

_____

_____

_____

*If you survived an abusive situation or a very sad childhood, how would you explain your methods of emerging from it and desiring a better family life today? What does that say about you as a person?

_____

_____

_____

_____

Designing Your New Family Genogram
to Create a New Legacy

If you could pack a family suitcase of parenting qualities for yourself, your spouse, and children over the next few weeks, which ones would you pack?

_____

_____

_____

_____

_____

_____

_____

_____

How will you specifically begin to interact with your family so that it will accept and see you differently?

_____

_____

_____

_____

_____

_____

_____

_____

Congratulations, you have just explored your history and possibly uncovered new ideas for your family and decided to eliminate strategies that do not fit your desired family life! With your history, remember, you are now the author(s) who are capable of creating a story your children may choose to copy in their futures. Keep the possibility in mind that each time you interact with your spouse, child, adolescent, you give them a glimpse of a parenting style . . . and make it a style that works.

Personal Survey

In the same way that the engineer and divorced mother began to look at their professional qualities, I would like to now invite you to do the same with your family members. This can be an awesome task. Look into your own areas of expertise and invite the significant others in your life to join in the adventure. Perhaps while they ponder over your abilities, they too will begin to perceive you differently and act differently in your relationship. Your interest in their answers will make the first difference.

Exploring Your Current Skills

A checklist and fill-in-the-blank forms are included so you have the opportunity to explore your *current* areas of expertise that could change and enhance your family life. You are encouraged to make several copies of the form and to give it to your spouse, a friend, two co-workers, and each of your children (if they are old enough to write). The more information you have, the better your understanding of your impact on others.

Personal Survey

A. List below the qualities, habits, and skills required to perform your job efficiently (*examples:* promptness, organized, skillful with client relationships, clever, etc.). Next to each quality, briefly note "how I manage to show this quality." (What I am thinking about, doing, showing others, etc.)

1. _____

2. _____

3. _____

4. _____

5. _____

6. _____

7. _____

8. _____

9. _____

10. _____

B. How my boss would describe my most valuable qualities and skills:

1. _____

2. _____

3. _____

4. _____

5. _____

C. Explain the qualities and skills you use when working with co-workers or good friends that contribute to a good relationship with them. Briefly note how you manage to show these qualities. (What do you think about, say, etc.?)

1. _____

2. _____

3. _____

4. _____

5. _____

D. Ask your spouse (or significant other) how he/she would describe your *behavior* when the "good times" occurred in your relationship with your family.

1. _____

2. _____

3. _____

4. _____

5. _____

E. How would *you* like your relationship to be at home with your spouse and children? (Imagine using a video camera and capturing a better relationship with your family. What would *you* see *yourself* doing that would tell you that the relationship was better?)

_____

_____

_____

_____

F. If you interviewed your spouse and each of your children, how do you think they would describe the *ideal* relationship with you? (Consider asking *each* of them directly!)

Hint: Ask him/her to tell you of a specific time when things were truly better for you and him/her. If he/she says, "I don't want you to *yell at me*," say, "Okay, what would you like *us* to do *instead* of that?" This will help you learn about new, desirable *behaviors* instead of hearing and focusing about old complaints. Additionally, the chances for defensiveness *decrease* when you say words such as *us* and *we*. This approach makes the conversation more collaborative and lessens resistance. Consider having a family meeting one night soon and taking inventory:

spouse: _____

_____

_____

child: _____

_____

_____

child: _____

_____

_____

child: _____

_____

_____

Solution-Focused Goals

Examine the comments you received from *E* and *F* and write these ideas for your *new behaviors* below. These will become your goals for changing your relationships.

Example: *I will sit and watch a TV movie with my son Eddie two times per week at 8:00 P.M. after his homework is completed. When I come home from the office I will take the time to talk to my husband about his day and help with the kids' bath so we can have time together later.*

Notice that the goals are behavioral and are *visible* to yourself and your family member. This is different than just saying "I will spend more time with Eddie." This *contractual* behavior is similar to job expectations. While families are not *jobs*, thinking of your new behavior as a requirement to produce change in your family relationships can produce a paycheck of harmony.

1. _____

2. _____

3. _____

4. _____

5. _____

Adding Solution-Focused Strategies to Your Goals

Chances are, many of the goals you listed have already been achieved by you before in other situations with friends or colleagues countless times! Remember, you are not trying to reinvent the wheel . . . only repeat what you and your family consider to be a better relationship in the past. Chances are, as you looked over the requests of your family members, you might have been surprised that their desires were simpler than you imagined. Congratulations, you have taken the first step towards parenting towards solutions and starting to keep problems out of your family relationships.

Examine *A, B, C* and *D*. With your goals in mind, consider the relationship with your family to be the most important job you have ever faced. Which of the qualities would *you* suggest using at *home, just for one week as an experiment,* to begin achieving the goals you have just described?

Please remember to go slow and *think small*, choosing simple tasks you can successfully complete for a week. Think about how you tackled a new assignment, project, or interaction at work. Then, list each quality below and briefly note how you could use the qualities with your family in relation to the goals you have set for yourself above.

Example: *I will watch a TV movie with Eddie two times per week.*

How: *I will prioritize the time with Eddie at home by scheduling the hour with my son two mornings a week for that evening.*

Solution-Focused Strategies:

1. _____

How: _____

2. _____

How: _____

3. _____

How: _____

4. _____

How: _____

5. _____

How: _____

---

*You may find that posting the feedback sheet will give you an indication of how you are doing *and* give you the opportunity to begin noticing how your family is responding to you. Place it in a very obvious place . . . and talk about it after the first week. Have fun.

Something Great Is Happening at Home!

The Family Feedback Sheet

Week:_____

how to score:

| 1 | 2 | 3 | 4 | 5 | 6 | 7 | 8 | 9 | 1 0 |

not so great   wonderful

A message to:	Score:	What you did that I liked:	From:

This week's most improved and enjoyable family member is:

_____
name

Concluding Comments

With all of your rediscovered competencies in mind, please proceed to Chapter 2. You are now on the road to change with your family history information, current assets, family feedback, and professional/clerical strengths in hand. Chances are, you have already changed your interaction and relationship with your family by doing the exercises in this chapter and your family's perception of you has also changed! You can now feel confident that the skills you have discovered in this chapter will not only help you to be the parent you have always wanted to be, but will also give your own children an opportunity to see you differently . . . as the parent you truly want to be.

"I find the great thing in this world is not so much where we stand,
as in what direction we are moving."

—Oliver Wendell Holmes

Chapter
2

New Descriptions . . . New Results!

"A diamond is a chunk of coal that made good under pressure."

—Anonymous

Peter, age 9, was troubled by school problems. His mom had taken him to be assessed by a psychologist who described him as "possibly" depressed. His parents had divorced seven years ago and his father had not seen him since that time. The psychologist who visited with Peter and his mother was concerned that Peter's crying spells at school were directly related to missing his father.

At school, Peter's teacher was very concerned about him, so much that she asked his mother to come for a parent conference. Frustrated with Peter's disruptive behavior in class and inattentiveness, she suggested that Peter was emotionally disturbed, for she had rarely seen such crying spells from a child his age. She also suggested that Peter had ADD (Attention Deficit Disorder) and should be on medication. This prompted mom to consult her pediatrician about ADD and her doctor agreed that perhaps Peter was very distractible, accounting for poor grades in spelling and reading. Mom began giving Peter Ritalin twice a day and while his grades improved, the crying continued.

Worried and concerned, Peter's mom described similar crying spells at home and a poor ability on her part to control her son at times. He would tease his older sister (age 13) and would at times become so frantic when he cried that mom would send him to his room where he cried until he fell asleep.

When I first met mom and Peter, I was impressed by the charming manner in which he shook my hand and was so helpful to his mom, who held his little brother, age 7 months old, in her arms. Peter was embarrassed by his crying behavior at school, saying that the other kids called him a "sissy." His mother was worried that Peter had a serious mental disorder, since she had heard so many descriptions from those whom she considered to be the "experts." I could tell that mom's worries were intruding on her natural instincts to curtail Peter's behavior and that she needed reassurance that Peter was emotionally stable. Whether or not Peter had emotional troubles was not the issue. According to Peter and his mom, they both wanted Peter to function in school and at home in an acceptable, appropriate manner. These goals became our focus.

As I spoke with Peter, he and I learned that his crying occurred when his teacher sent him out of the room, away from peers, or when his teacher asked him to sit in the middle of the classroom with his head down on his desk in front of everyone. This embarrassed him severely and seemed to worsen the problem. He told me that this made things much worse for him and caused him to cry more. His mother mentioned that the crying spells were also worse when his stepfather was traveling. When I asked Peter what his stepfather did that sometimes helped him to stop crying, Peter said that his stepfather would always talk to him after sending him to his room and would say to Peter: "I'm not mad at you . . . I love you . . . I just want you to be a better kid." Peter would then dry his eyes, smile, and stop crying. The other times when his stepfather was not there, Peter said it took him about 20 minutes in his room to settle down and then come back into the family room. While this strategy was less desirable for his mom, who wanted his crying to cease altogether, the timeout seemed to work for him at home.

This new information became a new description that I was able to offer Peter and his mom. Perhaps Peter was *not* "possibly depressed or emotionally disturbed, or even fatherless." Instead, based on the information given to me by Peter and his mother, he was "a bright, respectful child who needed time alone in a comfortable, safe place and reassurance after being corrected." He was also very close to his stepfather and a new description of Peter who "has an ability to become close to and respect a male in his life" not only brought a smile of agreement to Peter's face, but reassurance to his mom as well. As I shared this information with Peter and his mother, it was Peter who seemed the most excited about these new descriptions. It was as if I had freed him to think differently about himself as well. Then I suggested that there were probably some other people who needed to know our new "description." He agreed. He became anxious to tell his stepfather how important he was to him. Peter and I also agreed to write the following letter to his teacher, dictated to me by Peter:

Dear Ms. Smith,

I'm going to try and be a better student. I will start cooperating and listening to your instructions. When you have to correct me, please say " I'm not mad at you . . . I just want you to learn to be a better student." I will cooperate and sit up straight. If I have a question, I will wait until you stop talking to ask a question.

Love,

Peter

Additionally, I asked Peter's mom to mention something else to Ms. Smith when she took him to school that day. In front of Peter, I asked her to request that Ms. Smith do a favor for Peter, his mom, and myself. The favor was: *"Would you please watch for any times when Peter is doing okay in class and tell him so? Also, he wanted you to read this letter he wrote to you."*

Before ending our conversation, I asked Peter to watch for times that he could *show* Ms. Smith some new behaviors. Delighted, he said he could do that every day and wanted to start today. After two weeks, Peter returned to tell me that things were going great in class. "My teacher likes me now," he declared. He had changed seats and was ignoring peers who had taunted him previously. He had not cried at school once during the two-week period at home or school. His mom had tried talking to him calmly in his room when she needed to correct him. His attitude and his mother's attitude toward him changed drastically.

"Losing an illusion makes you wiser than finding a truth."

—*Ludwig Borne*

There Are Many Ways to See the Same Thing!

What was it that helped Peter, his mom, and his teacher to change their behaviors? Possibly, they changed their perceptions of Peter and this helped them to change their behaviors. Perceptions are created by information that we process through observations. This information is often so influenced by others' descriptions that problems can be created in the process. In Peter's situation, his mom's worries about the experts' opinions kept her from seeing him as a normal nine-year-old. Instead, she was cautious to say just the right thing and his teacher chose traditional methods to modify his behavior because she perceived him as emotionally disturbed, ADD, and in need of professional help. While everyone meant well, the methods failed. Together, they created a world in which Peter saw himself as having problems and things worsened. By suggesting and changing some perceptions, the following changes possibly occurred:

1. *Peter's perception of himself as a "sissy" changed to "a young man who feels better when adults reassure him." This enabled me to assist him in noticing other times when adults approved of him. He came up with many such times, raising his self confidence so that he wanted to show off new behaviors.*

2. *Mom's perception of her son as "ADD, a behavior problem, immature, emotionally disturbed and fatherless" became "a child who benefits when he is not embarrassed, and instead, gets some acceptance from those who must punish him." She was also reassured that her consistency in most situations seemed to work for Peter.*

3. *The teacher was not available for consultation; however, Peter described her previously as "someone who embarrasses me, sends me to people at school to talk to so I will settle down" to "a nice, smiling teacher who saw that I could be good."*

The focus of this chapter is to help you create new experiences for your own families through redescriptions and thinking differently about various problems. The new experiences you give your kids will change their perceptions, making it more likely that they will change their own behavior and respect you in the process.

Changing The Description Can Create Motivation and Hope

"The limits of my language mean the limits of my world."

—*Ludwig Wittgenstein*

If our perceptions of others can influence how we act towards them, then redescribing their actions (Epston, 1989) may also **change** our behavior towards them. For example, observe the following descriptions. On the left are some common words parents use to describe their children and adolescents when they are upset with them. On the right are some *redescriptions*. Which list would you like someone to describe you with?

Problem-Focused	Solution-Focused
failing school	isn't passing at this time
depressed	is sad sometimes
anger problem	gets upset at times
ADHD (Attention Deficit Hyperactivity Disorder)	is energetic; needs a place to focus /structure
isolative	likes privacy
defiant	is afraid of change, is not flexible *yet;* has his/her opinion; self protective
disruptive	does not know how to follow the rules *yet*

Problem-Focused	Solution-Focused
anxious	excited/careful
unmotivated	without a reason to work/get involved *yet*
irresponsible	hasn't learned to take care of things for himself/ herself *yet*

Changing the description of the behavior does **not** minimize or ignore the symptoms or complaints. Instead, it offers the possibility for us and our kids to see each other differently, relieving stressful, negative and unproductive thoughts (and ours) of:

> *"I'm bad."*
> *"I'm a failure."*
> *"They think I have serious problems so I know I can't do this."*
> *"There must be something wrong with me."*

> *"You cannot solve a problem with the same kind of thinking that created it."*
>
> *—Albert Einstein*

Eliminating hopelessness through redescription is half of the battle towards changing behavior. When my children were toddlers, I remember my very wise pediatrician saying to me, a frequent appointment maker, that "97% of my job is reassurance." As parents, when we reassure our children and adolescents that we see them as only being temporarily *stuck* (Durrant, 1995) and not problem-ridden, we are more likely to get cooperation and motivation from them. Referring to our kids as *stuck* also sounds less like a lecture and more like a dilemma that can be solved *together.* It makes giving consequences easier as well, since we see them as making a *mistake,* not as kids who have something seriously wrong with them. This consideration is helpful since it tends to make us feel less guilty and follow through with our strategies to help them be responsible.

Additionally, remember that a young child can tell the difference between being described as "a sissy" and feeling "embarrassed," between being "a slow learner" and "a child who takes her time reading" and will most likely act like the descriptions we and educators give them. Adolescents who need acceptance and validity often change their behaviors when redescribed as "unique and choosy about their hair" instead of "strange and weird with purple hair." The redescriptions lessen the negative attention-getting behaviors and give them less of a chance at becoming a problem in your family. Teenagers in particular have always enjoyed shocking and being dramatically different. One of the most humorous comments I have ever heard about teenagers, however, is that "teenagers desire so much to be different that they feel they must all dress the same!"

Looking at the behavior differently can also influence how we react to our kids when they misbehave disruptively, after traditional means of quieting them fails. For example, a parent once complained to me that her son, Joey, age 14, was a real troublemaker during weeknights at home when he was supposed to do his homework. Apparently Joey attempted to break the monotony of homework in the family by telling jokes, teasing his younger brothers and sisters, and playing his music loudly until his mom grounded him to his room to study alone. After a few minutes of solitude, Joey still came out of his room to do more of the same. When I asked her to describe Joey in a few words, she said he was:

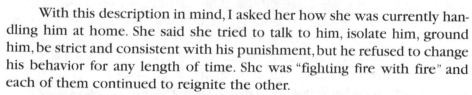

- defiant
- disruptive
- disrespectful
- inconsiderate

With this description in mind, I asked her how she was currently handling him at home. She said she tried to talk to him, isolate him, ground him, be strict and consistent with his punishment, but he refused to change his behavior for any length of time. She was "fighting fire with fire" and each of them continued to reignite the other.

As I listened to the parent describe Joey, I envisioned him being a challenge at home, but also as attempting to get his mom's attention and "liven up" the family through his sense of humor. Why else, after all, would a fourteen-year-old continue to make himself so "visible"? I asked myself and the parent: *"I wonder what it does for him to act this way?"*

Together, we came up with the possibility that Joey likes and wants "visibility" in her home. I asked her how she might act towards Joey just for an evening, if she began thinking about him as:

- a person who likes visibility
- a person who is very social with his family
- a person who liked giving/getting attention from his brothers and sisters
- a person who liked to liven up less-interesting situations

After a few moments, Joey's mother smiled and said, "You know, it's true. . . . He has always been sort of a ham in our family. I guess if I thought about him like that I would probably smile at his antics more instead of acting irritated, and spend time with him myself. The other kids need some quiet to do their homework so this might work. When he was younger, he was always at my side. Maybe I have forgotten how much he loved the attention."

After the initial experiment, Joey's mom made sure that whenever she saw Joey teasing his brothers and sisters, she took it to mean that he needed the spotlight or attention from them. She would then request that everyone stop and listen to Joey's jokes or request that he assist her with helping his younger brother to "liven up social studies homework." After a few weeks of thinking about Joey in this way, Joey required less attention and seemed to feel confident that his role in the family was secure. In a way, his mom stopped trying to mold him into something she thought he should be and cooperated with who he was. Together, they found a winning combination that worked for them to dismiss the problem.

Learning to See Kids as Inexperienced in the World

Using your newly identified skills from the previous chapter may now be easier as you consider using a redescription along with your newly identified parenting skills. Remember, the goal of parenting is to produce responsible, appropriate, respectful adults—and in order to do that, we must get our kids' attention . . . not their defiance. For years I have observed parents reprimanding, scolding and criticizing their kids, while the kids looked at their shoelaces in disgrace or screamed back in defense. The kids never heard a word. They were too busy feeling terrible about themselves and reacting immaturely, which was the only way they knew.

What *is* helpful when our kids misbehave, act immaturely or irresponsibly is to first remember how much longer you and I have lived in the world and how much more experience we have in dealing with problems and situations. Consider asking yourself the following question the next time you experience frustration: "How much does _____ know about situations such as this one?"

For example:

- "How much does Susie *know* about interviewing/dressing for a new job?"

- "How much does John ***understand*** about studying for the ACT exam?"

- "How much ***experience*** does Jonathan have that helps him realize the dangers of rollerblading down the street with heavy traffic?"

- "What dangers has Anna ***experienced*** with walking down the street at midnight after baby-sitting instead of calling for a ride?"

- "Did Timmy ***know how*** to play with other children before he was scolded the first week in his preschool class?"

Too often, we expect our kids to have the same range of knowledge that took us years to achieve. It is simply not fair to expect them to imagine certain outcomes, consequences, or results when they have not experienced them before. It seems more helpful to imagine how your child might feel or perceive the event before you jump in with suggestions. We are their first *teachers* and a teacher's role is to motivate students by creating an environment in which they want to listen and learn.

For example, over the past year our sixteen-year-old son has learned how to drive. As he and I drove together for the first few terrifying times, I realized how many precautions I take daily when I drive. When I began to verbalize to Roger, Jr. several of many precautions, I realized how much I had learned and how much he would also learn over his lifetime of driving. There was no way he could possibly know to take the precautions experienced drivers take each day. Expressing dissatisfaction to him over what he had little information on would have been unfair and degrading. Instead, I fastened my seatbelt tightly, crossed my fingers, and remembered how inexperienced he really was. This seemed to help me have more patience and act less terrified! It taught me to give him directions *before we arrived at the intersection* and compliment him before giving him advice. This resulted in his feeling more at ease, listening to me more often, and being a better driver *eventually.*

Usually, the children I consult with do not have the same concerns their parents have. The kids have not tried to see "the light" as offered to them by their parents, but their shame of misbehavior or rebellion to suggestions prevented them from considering the advice and left them defensive. Redescribing problems and seeing where your kids' experience level is is more likely to produce a better attitude and lessen resistance to your ideas. The focus of this book is to assist your kids in solving their own problems, with little assistance from you. They simply cannot do this if they are blinded by descriptions that cripple and shame them. The following exercise is designed to help you see where you currently are in describing your kids. Use it as a guide to change your thinking and maybe your actions.

Description Exercise

Identifying Descriptions and Responses That Are Currently Working

Below, on the left side, write several words that describe your child/adolescent's negative behavior when you are frustrated, upset, or worried. In the middle write *your* behaviors, reactions, or interactions toward your child/adolescent when you think about/describe him/her in this way. Place a check in the column on the right if your response is working to produce a positive result with your child.

child/adolescent's negative behaviors	parent's responses interactions/actions	are the responses working/not working?
1. _____	_____	_____
_____	_____	_____
2. _____	_____	_____
_____	_____	_____
3. _____	_____	_____
_____	_____	_____
4. _____	_____	_____
_____	_____	_____
5. _____	_____	_____
_____	_____	_____

*Consider **only** doing the responses that work for the next week and discontinue using those that are not working. If there are no responses currently working, proceed to the next exercise.*

Redescription Exercise

Applying New Descriptions to Negative Behaviors

Below, on the left side, write several new *redescriptions* of the same behaviors you were concerned about on the Description Excrcise. Think of *other ways* you or someone else could describe the same behaviors. In the middle column *imagine* how you might react/interact with someone who had *these* descriptions. Place a check after the new response if this type of interaction has worked in the past with your kids, your spouse, friends, or co-workers.

new descriptions for child/adolescent behaviors	parent's new responses	has this response worked with your kids, spouse, etc?
1. _____	_____	_____
_____	_____	_____
2. _____	_____	_____
_____	_____	_____
3. _____	_____	_____
_____	_____	_____
4. _____	_____	_____
_____	_____	_____
5. _____	_____	_____
_____	_____	_____

Are your responses different? Identify several to try for a day. Remember to use those in particular that you have been successful using with others as well as your kids.

Using New Assumptions to Think Differently About Your Kids

Once when I was consulting for a Residential Treatment Center in Texas, I drove up to the facility and noticed children playing soccer. Watching them, I remember thinking how *typically* they were playing and relating to each other. As I approached the director of the RTC and mentioned this thought to him, he looked at me curiously and said, "But you don't know what's wrong with them yet, do you?" He was right. I didn't know. Instead, I saw them as normal kids, without the prejudice of labels. I can't help but wonder how the children would have reacted to me if I had approached them, with my first impression being that they seemed *normal.* I wonder what *they* would have told me were the reasons why they were living in the RTC. I also wonder if there was a conflict between goals and assumptions set by the staff and those set by the kids.

New Assumptions for Parents to Use . . . Ideas from Solution-Focused Brief Therapy

When William O'Hanlon and Michelle Weiner-Davis wrote the book *In Search of Solutions,* they provided counselors with new ways of viewing their clients. Instead of looking *for* problems, O'Hanlon and Weiner-Davis encouraged them to see problems *differently,* focusing less on *why* problems occurred and more on when they did *not.* The next section will illustrate some of their ideas from a parenting perspective. As you read them, attempt to think differently about the problems that may bother your kids and consider new ways of handling them.

Guiding Ideas for Parenting Toward Solutions adapted from O'Hanlon and Weiner-Davis, 1989

1. **Instead of noticing only problems, look for the "exceptions," or the times when the problem is not occurring.**

   Parents often tell me the following complaints:

   "he's always hyperactive"

   "she is constantly angry"

   "she has been depressed for the past six months"

   "he's failing two subjects"

These are statements that exclude "exceptions," the times when people are not bothered by their problems. Consider the following "exceptions":

- If a young boy is constantly hyperactive, he would surely be exhausted, yet he typically is not! "Energetic" kids tend to be less energetic when they are in a quiet place with few distractions, focusing on something visual. An energetic child probably completes his homework better in a quiet place with a parent sitting in the same room to keep him on track. Just because he needs this constant assistance does not mean it is problematic. It is simply helpful.

- A young girl who seems "constantly angry" may take breaks and enjoy her friends, attend school, try out for track, and talk to her friends on the phone. Her anger when she talks to her mother may occur for a total of 30 minutes per day. It is helpful to examine what might be going on in those other activities that seems to free her from "anger," or, to watch what mom and daughter are doing during the interactions where anger is not present.

- A sixteen-year-old whom someone may describe as depressed "all of the time" often continues to attend school, live with her family, and participate in activities when her honors classes are less stressful. If the "depression" that bothered her completely took over, she would probably not get out of bed. Yet, she does. It may be interesting to keep track of the days when the "depression" is less, leading to a discovery that perhaps next semester, less honors classes should be taken.

- The seventeen-year-old who begins failing two classes in March might find his secret to recovering from his "temporary failing" by looking over the past six months of successful passing. Additionally, observing his other five or six classes might give him ideas for bringing up his two failing classes. Merely focusing on "what went wrong" is about as productive as watching a football quarterback miss his receiver.

Questions that can be very helpful to identifying exceptions are:

"When is it that you don't feel as _____ (angry, sad, energetic, depressed)?"

"When is it that you have _____ (passed this/or another Math class, turned in homework on time, obtained the help you need)?"

2. Do not attempt to figure out "why" a problem is happening.

Understanding *why* your child/adolescent has a problem will only give you answers, not solutions. Additionally, too much searching of *why* something is occurring may begin to make your child/adolescent feel as if the problem is really bigger than it is.

For example, even in very unfortunate situations of physical abuse, sexual abuse and verbal/emotional abuse, knowing these answers does not free up the individual to proceed. However, mentioning to a young person the following statement can be *empowering* and assist with moving on:

> *"Tina, in spite of the awful things that have happened to you, I want you to know how proud I am of you to continue going to school, making good grades, helping me around the house. I'm not sure how you do it. Can you tell me? You are truly amazing and I am proud to be your mom."*

I wish for all of the young people who endure such unfortunate situations the peace of mind of being *free* from the events that try to torture them afterwards. After many years of talking to such people, this approach has proven to me to be more freeing and complimentary than any other. Reliving the horrible details is not always necessary to *deal with the abuse.* I would rather suggest to the young person that *the abuse is over and their knowledge will help to prevent it ever happening again.* By suggesting that they have already moved forward with the above question, young persons can begin to see that this is truly a possibility.

3. Allow your children/adolescents to set their own goals.

As parents, we have the knowledge of many years that helps us to know what we should do to solve problems. Kids do not have this luxury, nor do they always agree with us when we tell them what they should do. Instead, the next time your child/adolescent has a problem with a playmate, teacher, sibling, other parent, friend or is facing dire consequences, consider asking the following questions:

> *"This sounds really awful. How will you know when things are better for you?"*

> *"When was the last time you were able to get that to happen?"*

Chances are, even if this is a new situation—such as the first time your child is in trouble at school or with the law, failing a class, fighting at school or with their father—there have been *other times* when he or she controlled anger, walked away from a conflict or passed a tough class (even if a few years ago). Even if the goal you are given seems shallow, such as "I will get Ms. Johnson, the social studies teacher, off my back" or "Thomas will stop pestering me in my room," go along with it. The question to ask if *somebody else is the problem* is:

> *"Great idea. . . . What do you think_____ (Ms. Johnson, Thomas) would say that* you *have done before to get this to happen?"*

Or,

> *"What have you done before that kept Ms. Johnson off your back?"*

> *"What has helped to keep Thomas out of your room?"*

If you hear answers such as "I don't know, ask her/him," do it!

> *"If I asked Ms. Johnson what you do sometimes that keeps her from giving you a hard time, what would she say?"*

> *"If I asked Thomas what you did sometimes that kept him from wanting to pester you, what would he say you did that helped that to happen?"*

The key to making this question work with your kids is to help them be specific by then asking them:

> *"If I followed you around with my video camera for the next week when you were on top of this problem, what would I see you doing when I played back the tape? How would it be different from what just happened when the problem was in charge of you?"*

As your kids begin to tell you *specifically* what they will be doing, add your own observations of their past successes. Perhaps you recall days when your older son and his sister got along famously. Recall aloud to your daughter what you saw her doing that seemed to work for her and ask her, "How did you do that?"

Notice how the focus changes from how terrible the problem is to *solutions to stay on top of the problem.* Make sure to con-

tinue asking "What else will you specifically do?" so that your child/adoles-
cent has many strategies to use. Make sure you set the time for change at a
reasonable pace:

- For a young child, ages 5 to 11, remind him of his strategies *daily*, asking him to use the strategy *only one day at a time, perhaps only one
  afternoon or morning at a time*.

- For an adolescent, ages 12 to 18, ask her to use the strategy for no
  longer than a week at a time, beginning with daily use. Reasons for the
  short time span? Most of us can accomplish a new plan for a short
  time and be successful at it. Besides, lasting change occurs slowly and
  requires small steps.

4.   **Remember that complex problems do not always mean there
     must be a complex solution.**

As a school counselor many years ago, I recall working with a fifth-
grade boy named Steven who had a problem with encopresis (soiling his
pants). He would routinely soil his pants around 11:00 a.m. each morning.
His teacher would then send him to the nurse, who would then call his
mom, who would then pick him up, and take him home to clean himself
up. Mom was a single parent who was jeopardizing her job. She had tried:

- lecturing him on how his behavior was threatening her job
- having a pediatrician evaluate him physically
- punishing him for soiling his pants
- making him wash his soiled pants
- leaving him at school in soiled pants
- . . . and nothing had worked.

The principal and teacher were frustrated and
asked me to speak to him. As I spoke to Steven, a
slightly overweight young man, I realized that the
problem did not occur *every day*. In fact, the more I
talked to him the more I began to wonder what it was that *soiling his pants
did for him*. So I mentioned to him that it must really be a drag to have to
go home and get cleaned up with everyone mad at him. Steven replied:

> *"Yes, it is, but when I do, at least my mom makes me one of her good
> lunches before I go back to school. I like her lunches much more than
> the sandwiches I have to bring to school."*

I thought, "It can't be this simple." I checked with the principal about his qualifying for free lunches and was able to arrange for the young man to eat hot lunches each day in the cafeteria. Then, I requested that mom bring a clean pair of pants to keep in the nurse's office "just in case." He had one instance of soiling his pants during the next three weeks and, thereafter, they ceased altogether.

Complex problems do not often require a magician to solve them. More often, the key to solutions may be found in examining what is going on during the *absence of the problem*. The tough part is orienting our thinking so that we notice when problems are absent instead of focusing on their presence. Try asking yourself:

> *"When was the last time this problem had an opportunity to happen and it did not happen? What was going on, who did what, what did I do?"*

Or,

> *"What does having the problem do for him/her ?"*

And then,

> *"What else could do the same for him/her that would not cause a problem?"*

In this situation, soiling his pants gained Steven a hot lunch on days when he dreaded cold sandwiches. By replacing his solution with a better one, discovered by talking to Steven himself, the problem disappeared.

5. Step into your child's world view. It will lessen resistance and encourage communication.

Just for a few moments, glance back to your junior high or high school years. Recall the turbulence of passing in the hallways, the smells of the locker room, the fright at your first high school homecoming dance, the threat of Geometry. How concerned were you at that point about becoming a doctor, lawyer, teacher, businessperson, or plumber? Chances are, if you were like the typical adolescent, you were more concerned about how your hair looked or the dance Friday night. Yet we expect teenagers, especially, to communicate with us about their life goals and lecture them on what they should be doing.

While talking to your teenager is important, so is *how* you talk to him. If your goal is to talk openly with your teenager and he is refusing to do so with you, instead of thinking "What's wrong with him?" consider asking yourself:

"What have I done/forgotten to do that has created this situation?"

For example, a gentleman named Barry Cade was hired as a headmaster to take over a school near London that was plagued by violence, racial problems, and extremely low test scores. The school was in danger of closing due to the tremendous dropout rates and constant expulsions of students. Additionally, the staff had become so burned out that their first response to any student misbehavior was to send them to the office.

Mr. Cade's first task after he arrived at the school was to speak to the teachers regarding his role as a disciplinarian. He basically told them that he would no longer be there to solve their problems. When a situation occurred between a teacher and student, the teacher was to ask herself:

"What have I done to create this situation? What did I not do that could have prevented it?"

Mr. Cade lost 50 percent of his faculty very quickly. However, after he hired new faculty members with this mindset, his school rose to the top in test scores, the violence and expulsions ceased completely, and the school population increased. His first priority for the school was: "The students must feel good about themselves."

Stepping into your child/adolescent's world view means just that . . . "they must feel good about themselves" in order to communicate, be motivated, and take action towards better behavior. This does not mean that parents need to stop giving consequences, but it does mean that placing ourselves in the shoes of our kids will give us clues to talking to them so they will listen and solve their own problems. We can then give them consequences that are contingent on their behavior changing.

I learned this lesson first hand, recently, when my fourteen-year-old daughter, Kelli, met a sixteen-year-old male at a school activity recently and he began to call her frequently on the phone. At first she was reluctant to tell me about him, saying that he was just a friend. Typically she talks to me non-stop about her friends so I was puzzled at her reluctance to tell me about him. After thinking about this situation, I asked myself:

"What have I done that might have kept her from telling me more about him?"

I then realized that she might have felt that I would say "no" to his calls. He was the first *older* boy who called her. I went to her and asked *her,* for verification, the same question. She said: "I know he's older than most of the boys who call me and I was afraid you would not like him calling me." I told her I understood that she was growing up and that older boys were becoming interesting to her and interested *in* her. I also told her that if she had chosen him as a friend, then I was sure he would be someone her dad and I would approve of. He could come over to visit her whenever we were home and call her when he wanted to as long as it was before 10:00, her phone curfew. She was thrilled. Since then, she tells me non-stop about her new "friend."

When things go wrong between parent and child, it is easy to blame the child's misbehavior or think that something is wrong with her. It is much more difficult to look within ourselves for answers. However, ways to mend relationships between parent and child revolve around the *atmosphere* we create as parents. Try thinking this way the next time a stormy problem strikes in your home . . . and ask your kids what it would take for the atmosphere to clear up.

6. **Focus on the possible and changeable . . . on specific behaviors, not emotions.**

It is very common for parents to consult with me over the following situations:

a. *My daughter needs to be happy. She sits around the house all day.*

b. *My son needs to learn to be responsible. He is failing three subjects.*

c. *My daughter needs to improve her schoolwork. Her math grade is terrible.*

d. *My son needs to stop being so angry at me. We can't carry on a conversation without his yelling at me and throwing things.*

e. *The teacher will be more satisfied with my daughter's behavior. My daughter is in detention each Thursday for talking.*

All of these situations deserve concern. The problem is, none of them specifically say what is desired, making it difficult for kids to know what they are supposed to improve. It is more helpful to think of these concerns in terms of the following questions and ask ourselves:

"What will I see her/him doing specifically when things get better?"

"What will I see him/her doing instead?"

This is more easily realized by looking back to the times when your child/adolescent *was* happier, less angry, doing well in school, etc. For example, can you tell the difference in the following statements that have been rewritten from the ones above, only more specifically? The *Solution Ideas* were developed easily when the goals became more specific:

Making the Goals Specific!

a. I will know my daughter is happy when she begins to play softball with her friends again next month. When she was active, she seemed more social and happier.

Solution Ideas: How have you encouraged your daughter to participate in sports before or encouraged her to join an activity?

b. I will know my son is beginning to be responsible when he does his homework on his own at least two days next week.

Solution Ideas: How have you helped your son be responsible before? What works with him? Does he respond to rewards, consequences, television time afterwards?

c. I will know my daughter is improving her schoolwork when she brings up her math grade by 5 points.

Solution Ideas: From your daughter's history, what type of help does she need to improve her math grade? How have you assisted her before? What would she say is helpful with math?

d. I will know my son is becoming less angry when I talk to him and he seems to listen to what I have to say without arguing.

Solution Ideas: How have you talked to your son, co-workers, friends, or others so that they did not become defensive? Have there been times when you talked with your son and you avoided bickering?

e. I will know my daughter is behaving better in school when I do not receive any phone calls from her teacher for a week.

Solution Ideas: What has helped my daughter improve her schoolwork or behavior before? Do teacher conferences make a difference? Does she like rewards or visits from me at school?

While it is still easier when your child/adolescent desires change, thinking specifically, almost *visually* can give you solutions to try immediately.

For example, when our younger, *energetic* son, Ryan (who is bothered by Attention Deficit Disorder), had difficulties turning in his homework assignments in fourth grade, I asked to meet with all three of his teachers.

One teacher out of three had no problem with Ryan. She had a tray on her desk and would ask routinely for all papers five minutes before class was over. Her class was also held in the morning, a time when he was able to concentrate fully. He always turned his papers in to her. After I asked the other two teachers to please remind him to do the same thing, his grades went up as he turned in all of his assignments. If I had said to his teachers, "I am interested in helping Ryan improve his grades," I might have received many different answers, including *"Ryan needs to become responsible on his own,"* something Ryan had difficulty doing at that time. By specifically discovering when *he did turn in his work* we all knew how to assist him. I then added a reward of a video game rental once a week, something he enjoyed, for turning in all of his homework. This intervention must have assisted him in structuring his routine.

Since fourth grade, three years ago, he has rarely forgotten to turn in a paper. He has become so structured in his homework time that he sets his watch alarm so he begins it on time each evening.

7. **Watch how changing the time and the place can change the situation.**

How many times have you wished for an extra ten minutes to relax when you came home? How often are *you* ready to discuss the answers to problems after problem-solving at work all day long? When is your best time to discuss a goal, pay the bills, express a need from your spouse? Chances are that the right place and the right time make all the difference in getting the attention you want. When problems occur in families, between spouses, and with children, in addition to asking ourselves "When does this not occur?" it is helpful to ask:

"Where can we go, what can we do, when can we do this next time so there is not a problem?"

When your children were young, there were probably places you would take them successfully and places you wouldn't dare take them. The same can occur with problems.

Terry Walkup, a school counselor, told me the story of Maria, a sixteen-year-old who often bickered uncontrollably with her mom about her curfew. One day mom came home early and *her* mom, Maria's grandmother, was in the living room. Maria and her mom had a conversation about the young man Maria was dating *without bickering*. Maria was in a group at school and relayed the startling change of communication between her and her mom to Terry. Terry asked her: "How did it *help* to have your grandmother present?" After some thought, Maria realized that she respected her grandmother very much and did not want to upset her with any screaming so she made a conscious effort to stay calm, to which her mom responded calmly. This led Maria to also add that she and her mom had held hands as they talked, something she liked very much. Maria desired a more positive relationship with her mother but had not been successful at achieving it until *a new time and new place* happened coincidentally. Perhaps the following question might have been helpful to Maria:

> *"When is it that mom and I talk, or have talked in the past, where we did not scream at each other?"*

Terry suggested that in the future, Maria consider talking to mom when Grandmother was present whenever possible. This keen observation on Terry's part suggested two things to Maria:

- She realized she and her mom did not bicker constantly, changing Maria's perception of herself and her mom, and helping Maria to realize she could control her screaming.

- She realized that a third party can be helpful and by thinking of how she wanted to come across, she became so aware that she held her mom's hand.

Sometimes when new discoveries are made, such as the ones Maria made, other "exceptions" surface as well. I often am asked by family practice physicians to do ADD assessments for children and adolescents who have disruptive or inappropriate behavior at home, and some problems at school. I do not use a checklist because I am more interested in the *system* they live within, so instead, I do an interview with the family and sometimes with the teachers. Very often, I learn from the kids and their parents that they do well in school behaviorally, paying attention when the activity is structured and routine, yet they misbehave miserably at home. When a child can behave eight hours a day in a school setting, it tells me that school holds *management* clues for his parents. This leads me to ask his parents:

> *"What does the teacher do that helps your child to behave and follow directions? When else is it that he/she behaves, is less energetic, and more appropriate? What is going on then?"*

These are crucial questions, for the answers tend to be of quite a variety such as "she's strict; she gives consequences; he likes her varied activities; she's calm and pleasant; her teacher pays a lot of *attention* to her; she gets a reward for good daily behavior." Whatever the answers, the fact that the child/adolescent functions appropriately for eight hours tells me *something is working* and ADD is not to blame.

8. **Continue to do what works with your child or adolescent. Stop doing what does not work.**

A concerned mom contacted me once to talk about her son, Ken, age 16, who was making the family life at home quite miserable. Apparently Ken and his father would have violent, emotionally charged discussions that left them both miserably unhappy. The mom told me that her husband had been reared with a very dominating father who demanded respect and hard work and gave no compliments or acknowledgments of his success. Her husband was an extremely creative and accomplished computer designer who had achieved beyond his father's expectations. Still, his father never acknowledged him. In turn, the mom said her son, Ken, a very sensitive adolescent, had given up trying to please his father. He never talked to him and avoided any contact at all costs.

As I met with the threesome the first time, Ken preferred staring at the floor to looking at his father. His mom remarked that she was often the "mediator" at home and was tired and exhausted of that role. His father badgered him during our conversation, forcing Ken to look at me and request for them both to leave so he could talk to me alone. As I met with Ken, he appeared scared and very angry at his father's lack of interest in him as a person. "I hate that I look like him, and as soon as I can leave home, I'm changing my name." I then asked Ken how he wished it would be at home. Ken told me only one desire:

"I want him to stop yelling at me for everything I do."

Then I asked him:

"What would you like him to do instead of yelling that would help you to listen?"

"How have you helped your Dad to not yell at you before?"

To this question, Ken seemed thoughtful. For the next few minutes he described how it used to be when he was younger and, more recently, when he and his father bought a used car for him to drive. "That was an unusual day, but it was good." I asked Ken what would happen if he had more good days like that day and he replied, "It will never *happen* so why even think about it. I'm just not good enough for him."

Afterwards, I met with Ken's dad and mom alone. I learned how much his dad loved him but was deeply concerned of Ken's *lack of motivation in school and at work*. I commended his father on having high expectations of his son, yet said I was disappointed that Ken was not hearing his concerns, only his criticisms. I asked him about *good times with Ken.* Dad could not recall any. I suggested that Ken (with his permission) had said he enjoyed buying the used car last week. "Did you know how much it meant to him to do that with you?" "No," his father said, "all I hear are his complaints." Then I asked him: "How would you like things to be with Ken?" His father said he wanted "respect, a good relationship, and to see him successful at work and at school." He added that he knew his son hated him. I asked him, with these thoughts in mind:

> *"How are you currently attempting to get respect, a good relationship, and help him be successful at work and at school?"*

Ken's father looked at me and said he knew he yelled too much, put too much pressure on him, and even hit him at times when he was angry at him. He told me it was the only way he knew. Ken's mom then said that her son was too sensitive for those strategies, and that she had tried to calm her husband, but now was so tired of the problems that she distanced herself from both her husband and her son. Saddened by what I heard, I asked them both:

> *"Would you say, then, that the strategies you have used to gain your son's respect, help him be successful, and get a better relationship with you have not been working?"*

"No, that's why we're here," they replied.

> *"What did work with Ken on the day you bought the used car? If I watched the two of you talk, drive the car, fix it up over the weekend, what would I have seen you do with your son that made him want to be close by your side?"*

Ken's dad had paid little attention to the fact that he had made the "good day" so important to Ken. After a few moments, he said they had often gotten along in the past when they worked on something they had in common. Ken liked mechanical things and his dad enjoyed them as well. Ken's dad commented that his son worked hard on the car and "got it running great before I ever could." "Really. Did you tell him that?" I asked. "I think so," he replied.

> *"So, when you work or do something with Ken that you both enjoy, you compliment him briefly and notice his expertise at something, would you say that you are accomplishing more of what you want with him?"*

"Looks that way, doesn't it?" The task I suggested to Ken's dad became clear:

> *"Would you mind, then, for a week, to try noticing other areas where Ken does well and also complimenting him when you see him successful, even if only briefly? In addition, how about arranging a time with him that you might both enjoy?"*

Ken's dad and mom left that day with Ken, who was quite curious about their conversation with me. I mentioned to Ken on the way out how I hoped that he would "watch for anything different his father did that week." Curiously, he said, "Okay." I saw the family one week later and the atmosphere had changed dramatically. Ken was spending more time with his father, had improved his school work and his job performance. His father had visited him at work at a local hardware store where he worked after school and had complimented him on his knowledge of his job.

Concluding Comments

> *"To think is easy. To act is difficult.*
> *To act as one thinks is the most difficult of all."*
>
> —*Johann Wolfgang von Goethe*

During the next week, choose only one time when your child/adolescent does or says something that angers or concerns you, and ask yourself how you are describing him/her mentally. Then, just for that moment, *redescribe* the situation *slightly differently* and respond to your son or daughter as if he or she was the most important person in your life.

Chapter
3

Creating Conversations Out of Chaos

Ideas for Talking to Your Adolescent

"The time to win a fight is before it starts."

—*Frederick W. Lewis*

I became acquainted with Kasey's parents early on a Sunday morning when her father called me frantically. The night before, his daughter, age 15, had left with some friends for a movie and did not come home at curfew. Her parents, concerned and fearful, drove around looking for her, eventually locating her in a local motel room with two older boys and a girlfriend. Through the smoke-filled room, Kasey's parents were appalled to find their daughter involved with friends whom the police described as "troublemakers." They were disappointed that she had lied to them about her whereabouts. The police had been called by the hotel manager and while the other teens were arrested, Kasey was released to her parents' custody since she had never been in trouble before with the law. Her parents grounded her for the next month and brought her to our session two days later.

My first conversation with Kasey and her parents was a chaotic one. Kasey described what she referred to as a "miserable relationship," particularly commenting on her mom's accusations and screaming at her constantly. She said that her mom often invaded her privacy and questioned her accusingly about items she found in her room. Kasey admitted to being wrong about being in the motel room with people her parents did not know but said it was difficult to bring her friends home since all her mother did was criticize them. At home, her father often tried to calm his wife during those confrontations but Kasey's mom was too upset to do anything but criticize her daughter. As the conversation continued to go nowhere, with everyone blaming each other, I began the following dialogue.

LM: "This sounds really terrible. You all have real concerns and the fact that you came here today tells me you want things to be different. How would you *all* like things to be at home?"

Kasey: "I'd like mom to talk to me, trust me, and not lecture me constantly. She lectures me so much that I won't talk to her about anything. It makes me hide things sometimes. Sometimes she gets so mad at me I just have to leave the room so I don't end up screaming as loud as she does."

Mom: "I wish she would feel okay to bring her friends around the house. I only want the best for her when I try to talk to her. I know I get carried away, but she's only fifteen."

Dad: "I wish Kasey and her mom would discuss things calmly. Kasey and I have always been able to speak about almost anything, but when her mom steps in, chaos happens almost immediately and Kasey contributes as much as her mom does. She and her mom are very much alike."

Mom and Daughter looked at each other, smiled, and nodded their heads.

The family's descriptions of what they *did want* instead of blaming each other helped them to identify the following goals:

- discuss things without lecturing; stay calm
- bring friends home more often

- trust one another
- treat each other respectfully

These requests seemed reasonable and quite obtainable, since at least for the moment they were able to agree on how they wanted their interactions to be, calmly.

I was impressed by how Kasey's parents were able to manage her between Sunday morning and our session. That told me she did comply with her parents at times. I then suggested to them that they all wanted to achieve the same goals. During our time together, I began to inquire about mom and dad's professions. I learned they owned their own business as athletic trainers, who developed and designed exercise programs for people in need of better physical health. I asked them how their "trainees" would describe the way they worked with them. They smiled and said they were "patient, consistent coaches who tried always to be encouraging to their clients." These techniques had gained them a growing, successful business. I mentioned that they surely must become frustrated at times when people did not follow their directions. Kasey's mom quickly said that it happened constantly but she reminded herself that those persons were new at the program and it often just took time to figure out the routine. She stayed calm during those times. The parents' strengths and competencies professionally were:

- patient with people in new, challenging situations
- good at coaching others to succeed
- encouraging to those who lacked self confidence

All of these competencies were dynamic parenting skills, yet Kasey's parents had not yet thought of using them in assisting their daughter. Instead of creating the same atmosphere at home that they did at work, they had separated the two and forgotten  to communicate similarly with their daughter, creating chaos in the process. Kasey responded defensively, creating still more chaos (often the only way many adolescents know how to respond to feelings of *rejection*). Grounding Kasey had little impact in the past, and since the mutual goal of everyone involved was to have a better relationship, it served no purpose but to prolong and perpetuate the chaos.

I complimented Kasey's mom on her wisdom to be a "coach" for her clients and wondered out loud what might happen at home if she used that same mindset with her daughter, a "new client in the world in need of coaching. " Since Kasey was in the room, I asked her what she thought about the idea and she said her dad already was a sort of coach, which was why she and he got along so well. I then asked Kasey and her parents the following:

LM: "Can you tell me a time when you all were able to communicate slightly better, talk more, and feel more respectful of each other?"

Kasey's mom responded first, saying she could remember just last year how she and her daughter liked to work out together, go shopping together, and enjoy each other's company. It was after Kasey's friends changed that their relationship changed as well. I learned that Kasey had made good grades, had good friends, and participated well at home until now. Kasey's dad said he always tried to be patient and careful with how he approached Kasey when he was upset with her in the past. According to him, she always seemed to respond better when he questioned her curiously, avoiding accusing her about an item he found. It seemed that her dad thought first and talked second, often asking Kasey what she thought as they began discussions. He said he found that giving consequences was easier this way. Their additional new strategies were:

- Kasey's parents would ask her how she felt about a situation before expressing concern and would then together discuss what needed to change.
- Kasey's parents would try to stay patient when talking to Kasey, and she in turn would try to stay patient as well.
- Mom and Kasey would spend more time trying to enjoy each other as they had previously and respect each other's privacy.

As the conversation ended, I asked Kasey's mom to use her skill as a coach at home with her daughter for the next week and "observe your daughter as an innocent, vulnerable person who is less experienced than you are. Also, watch for all the times when Kasey *does* communicate with you in ways that you appreciate." Additionally, I asked Kasey if she would be willing to spend extra time with her mom, especially when she noticed mom's attempts to listen to her ideas. I reasoned to both of them that their past history of enjoying each other seemed to be an appropriate outlet for both of them and I wondered if they might be missing such times. Then, complimenting them all, I asked Kasey's dad to continue to encourage his wife, as he would a client, to try her best to coach one of the most important people in her life.

After several weeks, Kasey and her mom were conversing more regularly and Kasey began bringing her friends home again. She was on time with her curfew and was respectful toward her parents.

During our last time together, I asked the family how they changed things so drastically. Kasey's mom mentioned that she just began to realize she had not given Kasey the patience she needed to and began to think of her as a young lady who needed to be listened to. Kasey, in turn, enjoyed the new interaction with her parents so much, she spent more time at home and felt comfortable to confide in them honestly and bring friends home to meet her parents. I asked them:

LM: "On a scale of 1 to 10, '1' meaning your family relationship is unhappy and '10' meaning your family relationship is perfect, where would you say you were when we first began talking several weeks ago?"

unhappy_____happy

1   2   3   4   5   6   7   8   9   10

Mom and Dad: "About a '4.'"

Kasey: "Lower than that . . . about a '1.'"

LM: "Where are you now?"

Mom and Dad: " About an '8.'"

Kasey: "Yeah, probably an '8.' It'll go higher when I get to do more things!"

I mentioned that they had all made this happen, then asked them:

LM: "What would you say helped to bring your numbers up so much higher?"

Kasey: "I feel listened to and trusted more. She doesn't yell at me as much so I feel better about talking to her about things. She's asking me what I think once in a while."

Mom: "She has just been so polite to me, and she's enjoyable again. I guess I realized before that I was too pushy and screamed too much. I guess coming here finalized for me what I had to do. I had not thought about her as being new or vulnerable. I just had assumed that she *should* have known what to do and my role was to tell her!"

Dad: "My wife is really trying to be patient. Life at home is more pleasant. I get to be less of the mediator."

Smiling, the parents and Kasey left my office, successful at developing conversations that were productive by looking at each other very differently and relying on strategies that worked together, not against each other.

To Fight Chaos, You Must First Learn *Not* to Fight!

Changing chaos into conversations can be difficult, as Kasey's parents found, because it often requires doing *less,* something that seems quite uncomfortable in the throes of battle. Below are questions you may find useful in identifying your current successful, conversational skills with your adolescent:

Conversation Evaluation

1. Is my current strategy working to get across my concerns, worries, or suggestions to my teenager?

   _____yes _____no

2. When was the last time I asked my son/daughter what he/she thought about this subject?

   _____recently   _____never   _____always

3. When in my child/adolescent's life has he/she listened to me or responded positively to what I wanted to say? What used to work, slightly? (Go back several years or consider your *partner's* success with your child/adolescent.)

   _____

   _____

   _____

4. What would my son/daughter say I did that helped him/her to listen to me? HINT: Ask!

   _____

   _____

5. When and where does my child/adolescent listen or talk to me best? (In the car, after a movie, late at night, Sunday afternoon, after dinner, etc.)

   _____

   _____

Brian Cade, a father of three and family therapist who has worked with many adolescents in Sydney, Australia, offers his tabulation of the *Approaches That Usually Do Not Work* with adolescents below. Notice how they *fit* with the unproductive strategies used by Kasey's family:

Approaches That Usually Do Not Work (Brian Cade, 1994)

A. **The Unsolicited Lecture**

*lectures

*nagging

*hints

*encouragement;"Why don't you just try to..."

*begging/pleading/trying to justify your position

*appeals to logic or commonsense

*pamphlets/newspaper articles strategically left lying around, or
    read out

*the silent, long-suffering "look-at-how-patiently-and-bravely-I-am-
    not-saying-or-noticing-anything" approach, or an angry ver-
    sion of the same

*repeated and/or escalating punishments tend also not to work
    and often result in more of the same, or an escalation of, prob-
    lem behaviors

B. **Taking the High Moral Ground**

*"If you really loved me..."

*"Surely you could see that if you..."

*"Why can't you realize that..."

*"Anyone with any sense..."

*"Look how ill/desperate/depressed I've made myself by worrying
    about..."

*"I'll love you and stop being angry/walking out/refusing to speak,
    if you do exactly what I want."

*"I love you because you behave as I want you to and will for as
    long as you remain that way."

C. **Self Sacrifice/Denial**

*continually operating in order to keep the peace

*constantly "walking on eggshells" in order not to upset or to anger
    others

*constantly putting the happiness of others before your own

*continually seeking to justify yourself

protecting others from the consequences of their actions

*putting your own life permanently on hold; hoping the other will
     change*

continually trying to please somebody/everybody

D. Do it Spontaneously!

*Where one person, through any of the above approaches, tries to
make another do something or adopt a different attitude, but demands
also that they should do it because they WANT to do it.*

"You ought to want to please me!"

*"I would like you to show more affection, but I'll only accept it if
     you do it because you want to!"*

*"It's not enough that you help with the washing-up; I would prefer
     you to do it gladly/willingly."*

Cade summarizes his findings with the following statement:

> *"Trying to make somebody more responsible, more expressive,
> more reasonable ... is an invitation for them to be obedient to your
> definitions of how they should be, regardless of your actual inten-
> tions. It rarely, if ever, works. The best you will get is obedience; by
> far the most likely response will be an increasing inability to
> respond, disobedience, anger, withdrawal, failure, resentment ..."*
> *(Cade, p. 10, 1994).*

Guiding Questions to Solution-Focused Conversations

The following questions may serve as guidelines when you need to
approach your teenager for a more productive conversation in the near
future. The questions focus on: (a) setting a goal, (b) identifying when the
problem does not exist, (c) strategies that kept the problem away in the
past, and (d) plan for the week.

1. "I need your help with something. I'm worried/concerned about you
    (the problem) and I know you are not happy with it either. How
    would you like things to be?"

2. "When was the last time you were able to do that? Let's go back to times
    when the problem did not happen. Can you remember? I recall ... when
    you were able to ..." (similar situations of success)

3. "What did you or I do that helped that to happen? If we watched a rerun of that day, that year, that time, what do you think you or I would be doing differently from now?"

4. "So, after thinking about what you want, what do you think you might try for the next week to make things just slightly better? What do you think I might do that would be helpful to you?"

5. "If I had a scale with 1 to 10 on it, and '1' meant the problem was in charge of you and a '10' meant you were in charge, where would you say you are now? Where would you like to be by next week? How will you do that?"

---

1   2   3   4   5   6   7   8   9   10

Why This Approach "Works" With Adolescents

In all of our developmental stages as human beings, there is no stage so emotionally fragile as that of adolescence. Adolescents have desperate emotional and mental needs to be loved, respected, validated, and accepted for who they are *unconditionally.* This is why their friends become more important than their family members after their thirteenth birthday. Many parents who know this are able to tolerate purple hair, odd make-up, colorful and creative clothing to a certain extent, because they know this is important to their kids. They refrain from criticisms and see their kids as the children they raised, not as someone they must conform and reform.

In turn, adolescents who *know* their parents are *there for them* no matter what, whose parents arrange their schedule to accommodate what is important to them, and tell them that they love them in spite of their low Algebra grade, tend to have less rebellious kids. These families also have less of a problem with giving out consequences because their adolescents *feel loved, accepted and validated.* They do not have to spend their time rebelling against the rules (which seems to be the adolescent's solution to feeling unloved, unaccepted, and invalidated). These families do not simply accommodate all of their adolescent's needs, they *cooperate* with their needs. Cooperation breeds more cooperation.

Finding New Ways to Cooperate

The approach used with Kasey and all of the ideas in this chapter offer ways to enlist your adolescent's cooperation and help you to develop productive conversations. One of the reasons this approach is so effective is because it encourages you to ask for your *adolescent's* opinion on how he wants his future to be instead of telling him how it *needs to be.* Additionally, using this approach, you do not ask your adolescent to *do anything new!* By looking backwards, towards more successful times, you literally become a historian for your teenager, reminding him/her when life worked and what they did that made it work. Then, by your recalling your successful times with him/her, you participate in the solution . . . making it less of a chance that your adolescent feels blamed . . . a feeling that often invites rebellion and defiance.

Recently, a sincere father who was worried about his teenage daughter's choice of friends confided to me that, as a youth counselor at church, "all of these kids talk to me about their parents, their girlfriends, boyfriends—and my daughter can't talk to me. I don't understand it. . . . I could help her if she would just open up." I'm sure he could, but what his daughter really wanted, according to our conversation, was to be trusted that she made good choices, and indeed, it sounded as if she had. She was able to stay drug free around drugs on occasion, kept her curfew, made all A's in school, and did volunteer work. It would have probably been more effective if her father had seen her abilities and complimented her on them. Then, he might have asked her opinion on a certain anonymous client he was working with, opening up a conversation with her and giving her the chance to feel respected.

Everyone Likes to Feel Important . . . Especially Adolescents

For a moment, honestly recall how respected you feel when your employee, employer, child, adolescent, boss, or best friend asks for your advice. It makes you ready to cooperate and be part of the solution, doesn't it? You probably feel so empowered you become more productive than ever. Even if your adolescent does not currently *deserve your respect,* give small amounts of it to him or her anyway and watch for the possibility of cooperation to emerge.

You have nothing to lose. To look past the negative behaviors you may only be able to see at the moment, consider think-

ing of your teenager as once the infant you cradled in your arms and promised the world to. Today is really no different—her body is taller, more mature, yet inside her is still the infant you bore. Thinking of her that way today or tomorrow, even if momentarily, probably brings a smile to your face as you remember the dolls, visits on your lap, or the angelic way she looked as she slept in her bed. This new way of thinking or recalling may assist you in responding differently and respectfully, even if only for this evening. I can promise things will not get worse—only better when you change your approach ever so slightly!

Make Parenthood a Daily Thing

The tough part in changing our behaviors and perceptions towards our kids is seeing past the misbehavior so you can identify what the misbehavior is *doing* for your adolescent. For example, many of us have heard the phrase "she's just doing it for attention" or "he will do anything, even negative, to get our attention." How true. If an adolescent needs attention, give it to him; denying him attention as a punitive measure will *not* work.

Adolescents who, instead, are restricted, scolded, disliked, and scorned by their parents look for acceptance elsewhere, and are often lead into dangerous situations with drugs, alcohol, and gangs. Whenever I have asked a gang member, *"What does being in the gang do for you?"* I usually will get a reply such as, " I feel like a part of something." If I ask (and I *always* do) a teen involved with drugs, *"What does smoking pot do for you?"* I learn from him/her what they need different in their lives. Then, I can ask:

> *"Tell me about some other times when you felt almost as good, but you were doing something more legal, safe, acceptable to others."*

The answers may become alternative solutions to the adolescent's needs which we can then begin to discuss in a more productive, less hostile manner.

In short, an adolescent's family holds the cards to helping him/her belong in the world. This is the difficult part of parenthood—creating an atmosphere in which our kids know that we believe in them, yet placing reasonable values and limits on them that they can follow. The chances are greater that the adolescent will follow his/her own advice and learn "what works" for him/her in the process.

The Experts Speak Out!

As I wrote this chapter on developing conversations, it occurred to me that the best resource for information were adolescents who were already successful socially, respectful of their parents, motivated in school, and responsible with their lives. The adolescent group I chose was randomly composed of males and females, ages 13 to 16. They were chosen for their positive, helpful behaviors at home and school, good academic performance, and involvement in community and school activities.

My goal in interviewing them was to glance into their family lives and learn from *them* what their parents did, if anything, that created a context in which they could grow up healthy and emotionally sound and motivated to succeed. Their answers may surprise you. On the next few pages are the answers to several questions I consider common situations faced by families of adolescents as they attempt to rear them into young adults. As you read through the dialogue, watch for the common themes which seem to develop.

Incidentally, I would like to thank these *amazing* adolescents for their answers and to congratulate their parents on assisting in their development as fine human beings. I am honored to know you all.

The Experts Speak Out on What Works!
Interviews With Adolescents, ages 13 to 16

1. **If your parents were concerned about your grades, what would/could they do to encourage you to improve?**

   "In junior high they grounded me but now that I'm in high school they leave it up to me. That makes me want to please them. I don't like to be punished."

   "I failed a class once and they just told me that I might end up like a garbage man or in some other low-paying job that wouldn't make much money."

   "They tell us what might happen if we keep on failing ..."

   "They take away a privilege for a couple of weeks...not any longer than that. Then all I have left to do is homework ... that gets boring and I'd rather watch TV so I do better."

"They don't mind if we struggle, but they would rather we asked for help. They are really active in our schedule and they know what we're doing. We talk about school daily and then help us with it. They have certain standards for us but they only want us to try."

"I'm a cheerleader so I want to do well. My parents are successful so I try to live up to what they do."

2. **What would you say your parents do that encourages you to come home on time?**

"Ever since I was a little kid I knew if I came home late that I would be punished, so I just don't."

"I think parents ought to be strict from the beginning. . . . That way kids just know what they are supposed to do."

"I want my parents to trust me, so I come home on time."

"They always have gotten along with me so I just think it's the right thing to do."

"I see how worried they get when I get home late. I get a time usually and I call if I am going to be a few minutes late. When I do something wrong they get discouraged and that really bothers me to see them that way. I try not to do that."

3. **What would you say your parents do that encourages you to help out around the house?**

"It's just something you do because they're your parents and they are always there for you so you do it for them."

"They tell me to have it done by a certain time. They don't demand it be done right then because sometimes I can't do it right then."

"Like, they tell us to bring down our clothes; If we do we have clean clothes, if not, we don't. After a while of wearing dirty socks, you just do it."

"They bribe me!"

"I think if I can psyche myself up to do, say, the dishes, then the next time I need something, I know they will help me with it."

"They used to pay us but that doesn't work anymore. If our friends come over they ask us to clean the house for our guests. They are reasonable, though; the chores depend on our ages. Now my mom does most of it because she understands how busy our schedule is."

4. **Who do you talk to if you need help with friends (or boyfriend, girlfriend)?**

"I usually ask somebody my own age."

"I talk to my friends, no offense."

"You just don't talk to your parents about THAT."

"I talk to my mom first. I seem to relate better to women! My dad is a really nice guy but it's easier to talk to my mom or my friends about boys."

5. **If your parents wanted to stop you from doing something that might hurt you, what could they say that would make you listen to them?**

"Tell me to 'think before you do things.'"

"Say: 'If you do this, this may happen. Just remember, so you'll know it's your own fault.'"

"My mom gives examples and that helps me."

"Have a conversation with me and then leave it up to me. There have been a lot of examples lately where kids my age got hurt or killed. My parents take on their role as a parent and say, 'This is what we think.' If they feel really strong about it, they push until I do what they think I should do. I let them because I respect them."

"They would probably say you're not just killing you but you're killing us. It's hurting you and it's hurting me. That makes me really listen."

6.   **What do your parents do that makes you feel important?**

"They say 'you did a good job,' or, that they're proud of me."

"Encourage us."

"Come to our sports games."

"Help us with homework; do little things that you don't notice at first, then later you do and you go, 'oh, wow, they took that much time for me.'"

"They say, if you keep up this good work, you'll get to take the boat out."

"When we do something they get really excited for us and with us. I had something really nice happen to me lately and they took me out to dinner, bought me flowers and a present. They get excited and make a big deal about it."

7.   **What do your parents do that makes you respect them?**

"I understand that parents are your parents and they're always looking out for what's best for you. So many of my friends have really messed up their lives and their parents just keep bringing them down."

"The church atmosphere helps. My mom's side of the family is really big in church. The difference is a different kind of love ... something that your parents give out. You see a difference."

"Sometimes kids don't understand life. Then their parents knock them down and push too hard. The kids jump into the muck with them. Parents try to take the place of the kids' friends and they just can't do that."

"In some families, parents end up creating guilt.... They say, 'Why can't you be like your sister/brother,' then the kids keep on getting in trouble because they feel low in self esteem."

"I notice how hard they work."

"There are a lot of us, and it takes a lot to put food on the table. I think a lot of that."

"They buy me a car, and there are a lot of kids in my family. They pay my insurance."

"They respect me."

"They don't pry. They knock before they come into my room. They respect my privacy."

"They have been in the same situation that I get into sometimes and it's happened to them. They can foretell what's going to happen. They tell us why we shouldn't do something. They are understanding, caring, loving, not afraid to share their feelings and they expect a lot from us."

"If I do something, like baby-sit, they thank me. I feel they respect me."

8. **What do your parents do that makes you want to talk to them, confide in them, etc.?**

"We eat dinner together at the same time."

"Our time together at night is the best family time."

"They don't get mad at what I have to say when I tell them something I've done wrong. They would rather I be honest and open with them than hide things."

9. **Do you feel like you are asked how to solve your own problems or do your parents do it for you? Which is better?**

"My dad believes in learning from our mistakes. He lets me make my own decisions."

"They say, 'Do whatever you think is right.'"

"They say 'I strongly advise you to. . .'"

"I think how they have been around a lot longer and they must know what they are doing, so I listen to what they say."

"Sometimes when it's not serious, they will leave it up to me and say, 'It's your deal.' I feel more comfortable with that and better about myself if I do it on my own. Sometimes it's good to be able to go back to my parents and ask what they think about something."

"They leave it up to me mostly. I'm an independent person. They give me the pros and cons of the decision and let me make it."

10. **If you could tell parents everywhere how to raise happy, respectful, nonrebellious kids, what would you tell them might work?**

"Start early in disciplining kids. Give them space and treat them like equals/human beings."

"Spend time with them."

"My parents are separated yet they get along great. My dad lives out of state but he sees us regularly and provides for us really well. He helped me buy my car. Since they get along well together, my brother and sister and I are fine. It really helps if parents have to get like, divorced, that they get along. . . . It makes it a lot easier for the kids."

"It's pretty much like this . . . how your kid is shows how the parent is. You learn from your parents' behavior and if they do drugs or drink, it's the only thing your kid will know how to do."

"Don't ground them too long. If you're grounded forever, you just decide that nothing could be worse so you do something wrong again."

"I think it's good for the parent to give responsibility to kids and if they don't meet them, take something small away until they get it."

"Tell them first if they need to do something in order to get something. Don't just wait until they mess up. If you tell them what they have to do and they don't do it, ask, 'were you too busy, what happened?' Sometimes, you get sidetracked when you really meant to do what you were supposed to. Realize things from a kids' point of view."

"I think it's my upbringing that makes me look at my parents and say to myself, 'You're supposed to respect them.' Upbringing is everything."

"My parents are very involved in my life. Some parents just say, 'Just write me a note when you leave.' My parents want to know that I'm safe and who I'm with, where I'm going."

"Some parents are too involved in their own lives and not their kids. They don't pay enough attention to them. The people who are rebellious talk about their parents badly and don't want to come home because their parents are not involved enough with them."

What Are They Telling Us?

- Be involved in my life every day, even if only slightly.

- Get excited over my successes . . . my joys, and show me.

- Be my parents, not my best friends.

- Let me know you are there for me; go out of your way to show me.

- Be patient with me . . . I get busy just like you do.

- I learn from what you *do*, more than what you *say*.

- When you respect me, it makes me respect you more.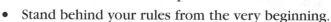

- Give me ideas for my problems and then leave the rest up to me.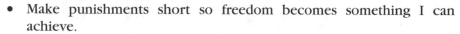

- Stand behind your rules from the very beginning.

- Make punishments short so freedom becomes something I can achieve.

Nobody Did It Better. . .

There are many theories that attempt to explain the intricate needs of the adolescent, but none I have ever read have said it better than the adolescents I interviewed. Parenthood is the most important job we have, yet it is often something we "come home to," "resort to," or "make time for." I had the pleasure of conversing with the parents of the adolescents I interviewed. The adolescents told me the truth when they said their parents were involved and interested. One parent said she wanted a copy of the interview so she would know how she was doing as a parent. This concern, sincerity, and desire to constantly integrate herself into the lives of her children came across in their matching dialogues.

Hey, Hey, Mr. Postman!

There are many ways to converse and communicate with your adolescent, and one of the simplest and most meaningful ways is that of writing him a note. I once complimented a father for finding his way back into his fourteen-year-old son's life by mailing him a complimentary note. I do this very often for people I work with. He must have liked receiving it because he decided to write his son. At a follow-up visit several weeks later, his fourteen-year-old—who had recently begun talking to him—told me his father changed everything when he sent him an e-mail message one day from work. The letter said:

Dear Tony,

I know you and I have had a rough time during the past few months but I wanted you to know how much I appreciated talking with you last night. I realize that I have pushed you too hard in soccer. I realized it when you cried last night and later when you told me how you had tried to please me without success. I am sorry. From now on, I want us to have more conversations like last night's talk and I want you to know that you have always pleased me... I just haven't always told you. You are important to me, and I love you very much

Dad

The son was delighted that his dad would take the time at work to write to him. The dad said it took only about 5 minutes maximum per day to write his son. Apparently this way they could talk more easily about "stuff" and their relationship continued to improve.

Remember the notes your mom put in your lunch box, the card your husband searched for, the drawing that said "I love you, Dad"? Remember how they touched you in a way that you never forgot? Writing notes to your kids when you notice the absence of "chaos" is as effective as six conversations later (White, 1989). On page 00 is a note to duplicate and *leave in a noticeable place!* Whether your child is five or eighteen, a note or letter is often treasured more than you might believe. Some of the teens and parents I have talked with have told me they *kept their notes in their wallets for weeks/months.* Apparently it was the first time in a long time that someone wrote something positive they were doing. It seemed to make such a difference that *I virtually always send a letter or card to clients after I meet with them initially.* This visual message that seems to say "I think you are amazing, competent people who will find your way back on track ..." seems to cement their motivation in place and remind them daily to try new strategies.

You Are So Amazing!

_____

_____

_____

_____

_____

_____

_____

_____

_____

_____

_____

_____
signature

How to Talk to Kids About AIDS, Sex, Drugs, and Alcohol So They Will Listen!

Important research was recently done by Miller (1985) in which people who were troubled by alcohol problems were broken into two groups. The first group was strongly confronted with being *alcoholic* and the second group was simply given information to read about drinking. The second group was more successful in achieving sobriety. Similarly, strategies that are helpful in talking to kids about such difficult, frightening topics as AIDS, sex, drugs, and alcohol can develop from using the same focus. When you feel a need to speak to your teenagers about subjects such as sex, AIDS, drugs, and alcohol, please obtain the correct information and keep a confident but open attitude about your beliefs. Feel free to tell your adolescent how you hope they will approach intimacy with someone they are attracted to. Don't be afraid to disclose your values and offer them as an option you sincerely hope they will consider. Most important, allow them to see your values in action.

Some of the adolescents I interviewed disclosed that they felt very uncomfortable talking to their parents about personal issues such as sexual intimacy, AIDS information, etc. Their reasons for being uncomfortable included perceptions that they were difficult topics for their parents to discuss. These topics are serious ones teens think about *a lot* but would never imagine happening to them. Their future consists of the next week and rarely beyond! Unfortunately, with HIV-AIDS, you deal with a deadly consequence of unsafe sex. Some teenagers think they may know their partner and may not question their use or nonuse of a condom. *Please give your teenager correct information and tell them you are doing so because you value their life!*

Your library can offer you the best resources for each of the above topics—just make sure the information is absolutely current. Additionally, the American Red Cross is an excellent resource for information on HIV-AIDS and provides community workshops for anyone interested in more information. You can find its number in your local telephone directory. The local Alcoholics Anonymous organization or psychiatric hospital in your community can send you information on drugs and alcohol, along with their side effects.

After you are ready to approach your adolescent on these subjects, set a time that is convenient for both of you to talk about an *individual subject, one at a time*. Watch for opportunities, also, such as a television show or a song you hear your adolescent listening to. Avoid saying things such as: "What a disgrace . . . I hope you would never do something like that!" Instead, say something like: "What does this show say to you about relationships? What do you like about this kind of music? What is your opinion on how quickly Sue and John slept together in this episode?" The following questions may assist you in these sensitive conversations.

Ideas and Questions to Ask Your Adolescent About Sex, AIDS, Drugs, and Alcohol

1. *"You are more important to me than you will ever believe. If I had information that might keep you alive, would you be interested in hearing about it?"*

2. *"Can you tell me what you have done* before *when you felt uncomfortable being around a friend whose choices bothered you?"* (Restrain from asking too many details.)

3. *"I was reading that many people do not know how HIV-AIDS is spread. Do you know? Would you mind telling me what you know?"*

4. *"I was really surprised to learn that one of the highest rising percentages of people who are getting HIV-AIDS are teenagers. What do you think about this? When do you think it is okay to have sex? How do you view your values on this subject?"*

5. *"What do you think about people who have unprotected sex?"*

6. *"Imagine with me for a minute a perfectly safe 'scene' for a friend who was with her/his boyfriend/girlfriend. Where do you feel they could be so your friend was not pressured to have safe or unsafe sex? What else do you think might help them stay safe and unpressured?"*

7. *"What are your suggestions to kids who try marijuana or alcohol? What do you think it does for them to use drugs? I wonder what else might have a slightly similar effect?"*

8. *"Can you tell me how you say 'no' sometimes, in a way that works for you? How do you do that?"*

These are tough questions but they are important ones, for they allow you to understand how your adolescent thinks about these issues and give you the opportunities to express **your** values in an atmosphere that is more receptive. After having this sensitive conversation, *remember to applaud, stroke, compliment your adolescent for his/her views on the subject that sound responsible and knowledgeable.*

Your sincere compliments will encourage more dialogue in the future. When I interviewed the adolescents for this chapter, they enjoyed the conversation so much they wanted to talk more! If you feel embarrassed talking to your adolescent about these ideas, please contact someone who can talk in an open manner. Perhaps that person will be your spouse or partner. Also, consider that, at times, you may have to do things that are uncomfortable to you at work, yet you do them. Check out how you gently assert yourselves with others. Analyze your strategies in those situations. Could you use them with your adolescent on these topics?

Perhaps you came from a family in which talk about sex was taboo. Respect that difference in yourself, and look for "exceptions." Think about how you had to get information when no one talked about it at home. Is this how you want your adolescent to view intimacy? There have probably been many times when you had to approach your adolescent about a serious topic. How did you do it then? This time is no different—just different subjects.

Most important, how do you wish for your adolescent to see his/her sexuality? Your adolescent needs information to make good decisions. As the interviewed adolescents responded, creating the atmosphere in which they can talk about serious subjects such as these is easier when there is an atmosphere of trust and you resist telling them what to do. Perhaps your school or church counselor, minister, grandparent, or your adolescent's favorite older cousin or aunt might be of assistance to you to relay the information your adolescent needs if you feel you cannot.

Concluding Comments: A Challenging Assignment

Consider—only for a week—thinking of your children not as children, but as young humans in a world that often is not too friendly, patient, or tolerant of their ignorance or actions. Consider this young human as someone whom you want to be close to you, so you might share the wisdom of all your years. Think of new ways to gently guide her with limits that aid her path through instruction, not restriction of her growth. Finally, remember how the human responds to kindness, caring remarks, and affection. Then, just for a week, show your adolescent that even on the most difficult days of all, you are there for her.

"If you judge people, you have no time to love them."

—*Mother Teresa*

Chapter
4

The Problem
May Be . . .
The "Problem"!

Ideas for Talking With Children Differently

"Making the simple complicated is commonplace; making the complicated simple, awesomely simple, that's creativity."

—*Charles Mingus*

Rachel, age 9, came to my office, accompanied by her mother, to talk about her fears. As Rachel entered my office, and I attempted to close the door, she jumped between the door and me, trembling and screaming, "No, please no . . . please don't close the door!" After reassuring Rachel that I *absolutely* would not close the door or do anything to frighten her, she sat down and relaxed gradually, keeping a close eye on the door.

Her mother told me that a year prior to our visit, her daughter had been trapped inside a restroom at a local restaurant for three hours. During the time when rescuers tried to jar the door open, Rachel became hysterical, beating on the door and making herself physically ill.

Until that time, she had no qualms about closing doors, riding in elevators, or closing restroom doors. Now Rachel could barely attend school without worrying that the teacher would close the classroom door. She refused to use the restroom at school unless someone held the door open, which had aroused many concerns with her teachers. On one occasion, the mere sight of an elevator caused Rachel to walk backwards until she walked out of the store and into the street.

Concerned that something was terribly wrong with her daughter, her mom, Jane, had taken Rachel to psychiatrists and other counselors in search of answers to help her daughter. Many of the specialists appropriately related the incident of being locked inside the restroom as the "cause" of the problem. Many specialists suggested that Jane should gradually close some doors both inside buildings and outside over several weeks in an attempt to "desensitize" Rachel. They told Jane that it was important to reassure Rachel that she was safe and would not be locked in again. While these suggestions made sense, Jane was *never* able to close the door even slightly without Rachel screaming hysterically.

I began suggesting to Rachel that it seemed that the "fears" had truly taken over and that I totally understood why she wanted to keep the doors open. . . so the fears could not lock her in. Our conversation then proceeded as follows.

LM: "Rachel, how does it help to keep the doors open?"

Rachel: "I can't get stuck again like I got stuck in that restroom."

LM: "I see. Does it make you feel safer, by some chance?"

Rachel: "Yes."

LM: "That makes perfect sense. How does *that* help, to know you are safer?"

Rachel: "It tells me I can get out."

LM: "Gee, I agree with you . . . knowing how to get out is really important. Tell me, how far can I close this door before the 'fears' take over and try to lock you in? Tell me when to stop, okay?" (I slowly pushed the door towards the door jamb at this point.)

Rachel: "Now, now . . . stop there . . . please."

LM: "Okay . . . let me see, this door is about 4 inches from shutting. I can see daylight . . . do you?"

Rachel: "Yes."

LM: "Rachel, can you think back to a time when the 'fears' were around, made you frightened, and then they slowly let go of you and you were able to be calm?"

Rachel: "No."

Jane: "I remember. Once, she and I were climbing several levels of stairs inside a huge building. Each level we climbed, she got more and more anxious. She became wide-eyed and her heart was pounding so fast that she became dizzy. She began crying and clinging to me. Once we saw the last flight of stairs and that the door was open, she calmed down almost instantly and things were fine."

Rachel: "I remember that."

LM: "Rachel, that's amazing. How did you calm yourself down like that?"

Rachel: "I don't know. . . . I just know that when the door is open and I know how to get out, I am not as scared."

LM: "Rachel, can you and I go for a little walk? I want to show you something."

Rachel: "Sure."

Rachel and I walked around our office. She and I looked at every lock on every door. I asked her to tell me how each lock worked: the lock to the back door used a key, the lock to the restroom had a self-locking device on the inside, the lock to our file cabinet, the latch on the refrigerator and, finally, we came to the front door.

LM: "Rachel, do you know something . . . you and your mom have been in my office for 30 minutes and this door has been totally closed. Tell me, how have you stayed so calm, with this door totally closed?"

Rachel: "That's easy . . . it has a window on it."

LM: "What? Wow . . . you're right! How does that help?"

Rachel: "Well, it's like in my school. There are fourteen windows in my classroom so I know how to get out. Each window is bigger than I so I can climb out of them. Sometimes when the teacher *has* to close the door I just think, 'I can get out through the windows if I have to.' It still bothers me a lot, though, when she closes the door. Then the kids make fun of me. But the restrooms . . . that's hard, because they don't have windows."

LM: "You are really clever. So are you telling me that when you know how to get out of a room, the fears are very small?"

Rachel: "They're tiny."

LM: "Let's go back to talk to Mom. . . . You've given me an idea."

Rachel, her mom, and I spent the last half of our time talking about what Rachel had said helped her to be less afraid. The following are the "exceptions," or times when Rachel was less afraid:

a. When there were windows large enough to climb out of, Rachel felt safer.

b. When Rachel could see how the locks on the door closed, she knew she could leave the room.

c. Whenever Rachel saw that there was a way out of a room, she felt safer.

From the information given to me by Rachel, I asked Rachel and her mom to do an assignment:

LM: "Rachel, you seem really bright. You have given me an idea that may help your fears shrink. Would you like to hear what you have taught me?"

Rachel: (smiling) "Yes!!!!"

LM: " Mom, I would like you to take Rachel to a hardware store during the next two weeks and examine with her every lock in the store. Rachel, I want you to become a 'lock expert.' You seem to know how they lock you in, but I don't think you know how they can let you out. Also, for the next two weeks, Mom, whenever you and Rachel go anywhere in public, as soon as you enter the place, I want you to examine how the locks to the doors of the building work, and count how many windows there are. Please, do not proceed until Rachel can tell you how they all work."

Rachel's mom was slightly concerned about the restroom at home as well. As Rachel and I continued to talk about her new, upcoming expertise of being a "lock expert," I asked Rachel what she thought could be the smallest amount of light she needed to see through the door of the restroom. She held her two fingers together very close . . . about $1/4$ inch apart. I happened to have a cardboard box in my office that day so I said, "Oh, about the thickness of cardboard?" She nodded. I cut a small square of cardboard and asked Rachel to put her name on it.

LM: "Rachel, take this cardboard and use it to measure the distance between the door and the wall when you go to the restroom. Use it to keep you safe."

Rachel: "You know what? I could probably just put it between the door and the wall, right on the place where the lock closes."

LM: "Are you serious? What a grand idea! Tell you what. . . when I see you again, I will be very anxious to hear where else you choose to use this. We'll call it 'Rachel's fear buster card,' okay?"

Rachel: "Yes!"

Rachel and her mother left the office that day and her mother commented as she left that the way I talked to her daughter was very different . . . as if Rachel was normal. She said she would try talking to her that way as well over the next two weeks, instead of asking Rachel what was wrong whenever she was fearful.

Two weeks later, Rachel returned to my office and closed my door behind her, grinning from ear to ear. She reported having a great two weeks at school and her mother said that Rachel was really getting into the "lock expert" role. She was still slightly fearful of the restrooms at school (no real locks or windows were visible) but she was allowing a friend or teacher to "keep watch" on the door as she went to the restroom. I complimented her greatly on her keen abilities to know in all of the other situations that she was safe. I did not mention anything about the restroom at school. I was more concerned with Rachel noticing her new abilities so she could continue to gain confidence rather than mentioning what she had not accomplished *yet*. A follow-up visit a month later revealed that Rachel was continuing to be less fearful, was going to school without anxiety, and was using public restrooms.

The following are the guiding ideas and solutions that occurred to me as I learned from Rachel and her mom what was helpful and what was meaningful:

a. I was curious to learn what leaving the doors open did for Rachel. She told me they made her feel safe.

b. I was interested in turning a problem-ridden description of "claustrophobia" into a more solution-focused description of "fears" and later, help her to be a "fear buster" so that Rachel could feel some hope and competency against the problem. I also desired for her mom to see her daughter as "normal" instead of having some sort of disorder. Changing the description accomplished this.

c. I inquired about any time when the "fears" were not so big. This type of question to a child is language-appropriate, since it allows the child to use his/her imagination and explain to me how much influence the problem is having on his/her life. For nonverbal children, this is especially helpful.

d. I wanted to align with Rachel very closely, agreeing how tough it must be to have the "fears" in her life. By talking about the "fears" separately from her, Rachel was able to talk with me about a plan to shrink the fears. By asking her permission to give her an idea that might shrink the fears, Rachel became part of the solution and I stopped being the problem-solver. This atmosphere is more likely to assist Rachel in the future with solving other problems instead of depending on others to do so for her.

e. I looked for the obvious. In our time together, I *always* try to notice if the problem a child or adult comes in to talk about is there currently. In Rachel's case, she indeed was fearful of my closing my office door. However, she did not realize that she was already closed in by the front door. Discovering the *obvious* with a child together is very exciting and extremely motivating. It tells them they can succeed again, slightly, because they are doing so now.

f. I began using what Rachel said "worked" for her—open doors, counting windows, watching locks—and went along with them, cautioning her to examine everything closely. In other words, I gave her permission to feel afraid. Sometimes adults who know better criticize kids because the adults know that they are not in danger. The kids have no way of knowing this and often a worse problem emerges from this very conflict! By cautioning children to take their time and watching them take tiny steps towards success, cheering and curiously asking "how have you done this?" the child is more likely to build his/her own confidence and proceed further.

g. When Rachel succeeded in all of her tasks but one, the restroom at school, I smiled at her and said, "I'll bet you will know when to be less afraid of that too. I'll be ready to hear you tell me how you will do that when the time is right." This manner of encouraging her without telling her to continue and accomplish that last feat seemed to be more effective, since Rachel could make the decision when she was ready.

Learning to Fight Fears ... By Not Fighting!

"Do not free the camel of the burden of his hump;
you may be freeing him from being a camel."

—*G.K. Chesterton*

The ideas I used while working with Rachel were developed initially by Michael White, a family therapist in Adelaide, Australia (1989). White talks of *externalizing* problems as a way to stop people from thinking *they* are the problem. When I first talked to Rachel, her mother had begun to see her daughter as having severe mental problems. This altered her actions with her daughter and made the problem worse. Even if Rachel had been "diagnosed," the diagnosis itself would not have presented solutions, just explanations. By separating the problem of "fears" from Rachel, she and her mom could band together to defeat the fears, freeing Rachel and her mom from thinking of her as problem-ridden.

For example, the next time your child is afraid, anxious, sad, frustrated or upset, *instead* of saying: *"Susie, this is silly, you have nothing to worry about."* Say: *"Susie, I can see that you are afraid ... the 'fears' are bothering you."*

As you do so, remember to interact with your child using your own successful strategies that you discovered in Chapter 1. Think of the places and times when you and your child are the most comfortable with each other and the "problem" is less likely to be occurring. This respectful, validating manner of talking to your child tends to lessen resistance and nurtures them into fighting the problem ... instead of fighting you about how real the problem is!

Guiding Ideas and Questions to Use When Fighting "Problems"

a. "What does the anger (fear, anxiety) *do* to help/protect my child?"

b. "When is the anger (fear, anxiety) not so dominant in the life of my child?"

c. "When has my child been angry (fearful, anxious) and then calmed herself/himself down? What was going on? Where was he/she that helped this to happen?"

d. "What do I do sometimes that may keep the problem around? How does my child, at times, lessen the anger (fear, anxiety) on his/her own? What have I done before that seemed to help stop the problem, even in other similar situations?"

e. "How can I cooperate with my child so that I can assist him/her in shrinking the anger (fear, anxiety)? How can I do this in a manner in which he/she feels it is him/her who was successful?"

f. "What name can *we* give to the problem so it *sounds* less threatening and more solvable?" ("fears," "the anger monster," "boogie man," "mischief," "bad days," "sadness")

Scaling Problems Down to Size

Not all children like to talk about the things that bother them. (Neither do many adults!) However, many children, even if not talkative, relate visually. Whether your child is quiet or talkative, number scales are a way of encouraging people to see where they stand in relation to solving the problem at hand (de Shazer, 1985). Consider drawing the number scale below for your child:

The problem is controlling me   **I am in control of the problem**

1 2 3 4 5 6 7 8 9 10

Then ask:

"On this scale, where '1' means the problem is completely controlling you and what you do everyday, and '10' means you are on top of the problem and it is not bothering you at all, where are you now?"

"Where would you like to be by tomorrow?"

"What would you be doing tomorrow when that happened that would tell you and I that you were in charge, not the problem?"

Many children love the idea of the number scale and will want to conquer the problem completely. Caution your child with a smile to not go too fast. (Often the reverse happens!) Ask him/her to tell you what he/she would be doing to move up one point. Remember to keep the actions very specific, behavioral, *and* include actions that your child will do (not another person) to change the situation. If your child tells you that someone else will change, ask:

"What will you be doing that will tell us both that you are on top of this problem, instead of it being on top of you?"

This is a very important question. If you talk about a *problem-focused goal,* you will talk about what your child will *not* do, and possibly, focus on blaming others. If instead, your child talks about a *solution-focused goal,* your child will more likely tell you what he/she will be doing to solve the problem. For example, observe the differences in the following goals:

Problem-Focused Goal: *"I want Tommy to stop hitting me!"*

Solution-Focused Goal: *"I will not stand next to the swing set at school tomorrow so that Tommy does not hit me when the teacher is not looking. Instead, I will play near the school building where the teacher and my friends are."*

Problem-Focused Goal: *"I won't get upset and cry so much."*

Solution-Focused Goal: *"I will take a break when I feel mad and walk to the teacher's desk and ask to get a drink of water so I can calm down. I will do this for three days this week."*

Problem-Focused Goal: *"I will stop fighting with my brother after school before dinner."*

Solution-Focused Goal: *"I will think 'the monster is bothering me and I'm not going to let him win this time.' Then I will tell Jody to leave me alone and not take my water gun."*

A trick to helping kids get to a solution-focused goal is to ask: *"What would you like **instead** of that?"*

Also, notice the short time spans included in the goals. There is a reason behind their brevity:

- "tomorrow"
- "three days this week"
- "before dinner"

These short amounts of time are important for they allow success to be more probable. Additionally, while using the scale with a very young child, if the numbers are not familiar, think of holding your arms widely apart, inviting your child to do the same, saying:

"When are the times when the problem is this big?"

"What is going on to help it be that big?"

Then, holding your arms closer together, ask your child:

"When is it that the problem is smaller . . . say, this small?"

"What is going on that helps the problem to shrink?"

This dialogue can be helpful and fun on a daily basis as your child becomes more in control of the problem. It is quick, fun and easy to do before bedtime, before school, after school, even when the problem is threatening to occur and you would like to see your child "win."

As you help your child become the expert on his/her own anger (fear, anxiety), hopefully when other threatening or challenging situations occur, the solution will be easy for your child to recall. Then you merely have to ask: *"What did you do before when the 'anger monster' almost took over?"*

For more clarity of this process, the worksheet may be helpful in conversing with your child about the following common situations. I have added additional "solution talk" phrases for you to respond with to help you get started:

Problem	**Solution "talk"**
• fearfulness	"We need a fear buster."
• lack of friends/moving to a new place	"Let's talk about how you made friends before."
• feeling left out/feeling sad	"What would it take to get the sadness to shrink?"
• forgetting homework/ frustration at school	"I think it's time for frustration busters."
• forgetful/disorganized	"Tell me about the times when you remember."

After working through the worksheet questions, check *daily* with your child about the progress he or she is making. Observe closely, yourself, for times when the problem might have previously occurred and didn't. Remark *curiously* on your observation to the child, asking: *"How did you do this? You are incredible!"* Or, *"You did your homework after such a long soccer practice? Wow!"*

Worksheet: Defeating Problems

1. *It sounds like this problem is really bothering you. If you and I could draw it or name it something, what would it be or look like?*

_____

_____

2. *What does the problem make you do sometimes when it's around?*

_____

_____

_____

3. *If you and I "erased" the problem from your day tomorrow, what would you get to do that was different from when the problem was around?*

_____

_____

_____

4. *That is such a good plan. Tell me, can you think back for a minute to a day when the problem (use the name) was not so big? On this scale, where "1" means that the problem controlled you totally and "10" means that you controlled the problem, where were you on that day?*

---

1   2   3   4   5   6   7   8   9   10

What did you do on that day that helped the problem be at that point? Is there something that someone did that helped? What did I do or your Mother/Father do that helped the problem to shrink? Were you in a different place? What was different in any way?

Child's actions:

_____

_____

Parent's actions:

_____

_____

Other Person's actions: (If another child, ask your child how he/she helped the other person to help him/her, in addition to what the other person did.)

_____

_____

_____

5. *If you and I were to plan an attack on the problem and not let it bother you for a day, what do you suggest to do?*

_____

_____

_____

6. *Tomorrow afternoon when we talk again, where would you like to be on that number line? When I take your picture when you are at that number tomorrow, what do you think I will see you doing that will tell both of us that you moved up?*

_____

_____

_____

If your child does not made progress at first, simply reply that the problem is simply a big problem that might take more thinking on both of your parts. Refrain from saying things such as "I guess you don't want the problem to go away." Chances are, your child does not want that to happen. Respond to your child with support, similarly to how you might support a best friend or employee. Comment on any other successes, *even if they only occurred briefly.* Mention that you are proud that he has not dropped too low on the scale . . . that tells you he is "holding his own" against the problem. Of course, if your child moves up rapidly, compliment him. If he moves backward the next week (a common occurrence since life is, after all, unpredictable), ask: *"What did you do last week that made the number higher?"*

You might even consider posting a scale on the refrigerator door so that you and the other family members might watch your child's progress. If you see the "problem" taking over, talk to your child about how "the problem" is appearing again, and remind your child to get in charge of the problem. Again, keep the progress on a *daily* basis for the elementary school aged-child and afternoon/morning basis for very young children. This helps success happen more readily.

Bring Out the Reinforcements!

Most of us enjoy some sort of encouragement or stroke when we succeed at a new task. Reinforcing a child's good behavior often leads to more good behavior. There are many ways to do this—gifts, notes, money, privileges, etc. One of the more exciting and effective means of reinforcing a child's behavior (ages 6–up) is the giving of a certificate or letter signed by the parent. The idea of using the certificate was suggested by family therapists David Epston and Michael White in their book *Narrative Means to Therapeutic Ends* (p. 192, 1990). Epston and White use the "narrative" approach as a means to encourage and reinforce what their clients discovered in their conversations. Additionally, I often write cards or notes to the children and families I talk with, commending them on their insight at solving their own problems, living through a difficult event or as encouragement to "watch for times the problem occurs less." In Rachel's case, I mailed her the certificate shown on page 97. I have included an additional blank certificate for your duplication and use. Notice that the certificate contains the child's name, the new name for the "problem," and the reasons for success. For maximum impact, consider making it a family ceremony when giving the certificate.

Certificate of Success

This certifies that

Rachel

has successfully defeated
her fears by becoming a lock expert.

She accomplished this by:

- checking out door locks

- counting windows

- using her fear buster card

Hooray for Rachel!

—Linda Metcalf, Ph.D.

Certificate of Success

This certifies that

_____

has successfully defeated

_____

by:

_____

_____

_____

Hooray for You!

_____

family member

_____

family member

Shrinking Problems Down to Size: A Case Study

"Life shrinks or expands in proportion to one's courage."

—Anais Nin

Neff Blackmon, M.A., a colleague and friend, once relayed to me the following story of Tim, age 8, who had been admitted to a psychiatric hospital for ADD (Attention Deficit Disorder) and violent behaviors. Tim had been placed on Ritalin® for behavior problems and poor concentration habits before he met Neff.

As Neff got to know Tim, he learned that Tim lived in a town hundreds of miles away from the hospital and was rather scared to be in treatment. Apparently, Tim's mom had experienced much abuse from Tim's father, whom she later divorced. After moving to Texas and remarrying a respectful, kind man, her life improved immensely until her husband was temporarily transferred to the Middle East. Missing his stepfather, Tim began acting out through yelling at his mom, teacher, and fellow students. At times he became physically violent with his mother and peers. Using advice from her pediatrician, Tim's mom tried a variety of behavior modification techniques without favorable results. She then chose to medicate Tim and hospitalize him as a last resort to help him.

Neff was careful to not talk about any of the problems that brought him to the psychiatric hospital and, instead, focused on Tim's favorite things to do. Within this conversation one day, Tim revealed that he liked to play soccer very much. On this rainy day, which prohibited Tim and Neff from walking around the grounds of the hospital, Neff took Tim to a recreation room that was not in use. As they sat on the floor, Neff began rolling a ball to Tim while carrying on a conversation.

The ball was red and Neff referred to it as a "kickball," approximately 30cm in diameter. Tim was able to focus on both the conversation and the task of rolling the ball back and forth. The conversation lasted 20 to 30 minutes without any incident of misbehavior. The following dialogue occurred between Neff and Tim as they "externalized" the anger that was *bothering* Tim.

Neff: "Tim, why do you think you are here?"

Tim: "I get mad a lot."

Neff: "How mad do you get?"

Tim: "I get really mad!"

Neff: "Who else knows when you get mad?"

Tim: "Everybody . . . Mom, teacher. . ."

Neff: "Are you mad all of the time or are there times when you are not mad?"

Tim: "I'm happy sometimes."

Neff: "What are you doing during those times?"

Tim: "Drawing pictures."

Neff: "What do you draw pictures of?"

Tim: "Animals."

At this time, Neff stopped rolling the kickball.

Neff: "Tim, can you tell me when you get this mad (holding up the kickball) and when you get this mad?" (Neff then held up a giant beachball, 60cm in diameter, that he found in the recreation room next to the smaller kickball.)

Tim: "Oh, yeah! (eyeing the beachball) That's when I'm really mad!"

Neff: "What happens then?"

Tim: "I get in trouble."

Neff: "So what are you doing differently when you are this mad (Neff held up the beachball) from when you are this mad?" (Neff held up the kickball.)

Tim: (Looking at the floor) "That's when it is still inside me."

Neff: "Tim, what could we do when it's this size (holding the kick-ball) to make it this size?" (Neff then held up a softball, approximately 12cm in diameter, and rolled it to Tim.)

Tim: (Looking closely at the softball.) "I could talk more."

Neff: "Who would you talk to?"

Tim: "Mom."

Neff: "Who else?"

Tim: (Pausing, then looking at Neff) "Dr. Stronks."

Neff: "Who else?"

Tim: (Smiling) "Theresa." (A member of the nursing staff)

Neff: "Who else?"

Tim: (Smiling) "Jenny, my teacher."

Neff: "So, when I come back in two days and I talk with your mom, or Dr. Stronks, Theresa or Jenny, what will they tell me about you?"

Tim: "That I'm talking."

Neff: "Can you talk to them when the mad gets this big (holding up the kickball) and tell them that you want it to get this big?" (holding up the softball)

Tim: "Sure."

As Neff followed up with Tim's behavior over the next few weeks, the staff of nurses, doctor, and technicians reported no more "acting out" sequences. Instead, they saw Tim seek out his mom and staff members when he became mad. Mom reported that Tim's behavior had much improved and that he would say, "I feel like that red ball's (kickball) inside," etc., which reminded them both that it was time to talk.

Keeping It Simple

This simple but dramatic idea used by Neff to cooperate with Tim suggests the following:

a. *Externalizing the problem of "mad" helped Tim to place it outside of himself. Neff then helped Tim to identify times when the "mad" tried to influence him. As Tim began to think of his "mad" as controllable, a new behavior developed ... talking to other people in an effort to shrink the "mad's" impact on his life and relationships.*

b. *Helping Tim to take responsibility for his "mad" and choosing a strategy that only Tim knew would be successful was easier for him to use than a strategy designed by someone else. Previously, he had been isolated in timeouts to modify his outbursts, but, according to Tim, talking was the best strategy.*

c. *Assisting Tim to realize that there were times when the "mad" was not present helped Tim to feel partly successful. This discovery allowed Tim to feel competent at least part of the time and to envision himself as a boy who could watch for the "mad" to approach and be ready for shrinking it on site. He now had a plan.*

Any objects such as variously sized balls, nesting blocks, different-sized piles of sand, boxes within boxes of all sizes, balloons, pillows, stuffed "monsters" and stuffed "kind animals", building blocks, stacks of books, etc., can be used to refer to as representing "the problem." This idea is especially effective and fun with very young children, particularly ages 4 to 9, and equally as effective with adolescents. As you refer to the size of the problem in your child's life, think about utilizing the following exercise.

Problem-Shrinking Exercise

1. Hold up the large toy, pile, etc., to represent the times when the problem is too big, takes over, and ruins their time.

2. Suggest and introduce gradually a smaller-sized toy, questioning gently how life might be when the problem shrinks down to size.

3. Ask your child if he/she can tell when the problem becomes bigger. Ask:

   "What happens when the problem gets bigger?"

   "What do you think you could do to make it smaller at that moment?"

4. As you finish, ask your child how he/she will do this in a variety of situations. Ask:

"Who else can you do this with?" Then, *"Who else. . .?"*

This information becomes your child's solutions and gives you a new, nonthreatening way of talking about the problem as well.

Disciplining "The Problem" With a Solution Focus: A Case Study

It is not often that I meet such an articulate, charming, and challenging six-year-old as Matthew. As he led his parents and eight-month-old brother down my hallway, he said:

Matthew: "Hello, Dr. Metcalf, I am the boss in my family. I have to keep everyone in line. . . . That means my mother makes mistakes and I have to help her, my father forgets things and I have to help him, I even have to tell my brother what to do. Actually, it is quite a job."

While I found Matthew fascinating and charming, his parents found him lovable yet frustrating. His mom reported that she could not control Matthew at home and that he was acting out badly in school, taunting other children, bossing them around and having trouble sharing toys and activities unless they did it *his* way. Mom had decided to put him back into a pre-kindergarten class at the teacher's encouragement, so that Matthew could learn how to play with other children his age.

Matthew's father had given up attempting to discipline his son since he found it unsuccessful to place him in timeout, scold him, or put him in his room for disruptions. Apparently, Matthew would throw his toys against the wall and talk back aggressively, often hitting his father and his little brother. Even the grandmother was refusing to deal with her grandson, saying he was too difficult to control for overnight visits with her.

My first attempt to work with Matthew was to suggest that there was an "anger monster" who bothered him at home and kept him from getting along with other children at school. When I asked Matthew to hold a "stuffed monster" in my office, I asked him what the "anger monster" made him do. He replied:

- get in trouble
- hit my brother
- get angry
- hit my dad

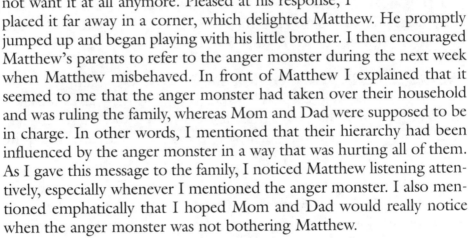

At this point Matthew became shy and with-drawn, and hid behind his mom. He gave me the "anger monster" stuffed animal back and said he did not want it at all anymore. Pleased at his response, I placed it far away in a corner, which delighted Matthew. He promptly jumped up and began playing with his little brother. I then encouraged Matthew's parents to refer to the anger monster during the next week when Matthew misbehaved. In front of Matthew I explained that it seemed to me that the anger monster had taken over their household and was ruling the family, whereas Mom and Dad were supposed to be in charge. In other words, I mentioned that their hierarchy had been influenced by the anger monster in a way that was hurting all of them. As I gave this message to the family, I noticed Matthew listening atten-tively, especially whenever I mentioned the anger monster. I also men-tioned emphatically that I hoped Mom and Dad would really notice when the anger monster was not bothering Matthew.

Visit #2

During our next visit, Matthew seemed slightly more self-con-trolled, yet Mom reported that he and his father were still not get-ting along in an appropriate way. Matthew was still refusing to sit in timeouts, was still hitting his father, and lashing out aggressively toward his little brother. As the family described the situation, I decided to talk to his father, a sales supervisor:

LM: "Tell me again, what it is that you do in your profession?"

Dad: "I am in sales. I have several people under me who I supervise."

LM: "I was wondering, have you ever had an employee who was not quite sure that you were the supervisor? For example, has there ever been an employee who was not quite certain who he was sup-posed to listen to, follow orders from . . . and instead of coming to you, chose to ignore you and do what he wanted to do?"

Dad: "Oh, yeah."

LM: "How did you handle that?"

Dad: "I just had to take him aside and get it through to him some-how."

LM: "If I watched you do that, what might I have seen you do?"

Dad: "Well, on one occasion, I took him into a closed room and talked to him calmly. I told him I was the boss and he had to come to me for instructions . . . no one else. I admit I had to be really firm with him and I had to keep on him so he knew I was watching."

At this point, I asked Matthew to play in our hallway where my secretary could watch him. I told him that Mom and Dad needed to talk to me for a minute alone . . . something parents often do when they need some privacy. While he did not like the idea, he gave in when his parents promised him he could have a treat when he returned. (Matthew's treat was to play with my secretary's type-writer!)

LM: "From what you have just described, it sounds as if you have the answer to solving Matthew's misbehavior and to keeping the 'anger monster' away. Are you interested in trying something really different with him?"

Parents in Unison: "Please."

LM: "Dad, I'd like you to imagine that Matthew is one of your employees for the next week. This employee is not quite sure what the rules are, who he is supposed to listen to or answer, and often does things **his** way, which jeopardizes your business. Remember, you have told me your success with another employee before. Use all of your skills at letting your son know who he needs to listen to. This may mean he should be introduced to your assistant-supervisor, his Mom. I'm not sure how you will do that, but I'm sure with some thought, you will come up with something."

Dad: "I think I know exactly what you mean."

Mom: "Thank you, thank you . . . you know he (Dad) works a lot and whenever he does come home, I do often see Matthew as more attentive to him, rather than me, at least for a short while. I really like this idea."

LM: "As you try this idea over the next week until I see you again, please notice not only how Matthew responds, but what you each do that appears to be successful in helping Matthew to become a model employee."

As the session ended and the parents struggled with leading Matthew out of the office, I wondered what might happen as the hierarchy switched at home. One thing was for certain: the family I just saw had many abilities they had not been aware of. The deciding factor, I thought, would rest within their belief that they were competent.

Visit #3

I knew the situation at home had changed when Matthew responded quickly to his Dad's suggestion of gathering up the toys in my waiting room. Walking down the hall in front of his Dad, I noticed a polite young six-year-old who then proceeded to ask me to use my pen, write on my paper, and put things back whenever he used them. What a transformation! I complimented him on his asking me for things and looked at two very proud parents who nodded at me with smiles on their faces.

LM: "Tell me what's been better since I last saw you."

Mom: "Everything. He (glancing at Dad) has just been wonderful with Matthew."

LM: "Gee . . . what would you say you are doing that is making such a big difference in your family life, Dad?"

Dad: "Well, I began by being extremely consistent with him. It was hard . . . it took constant watching. For example, if I put him in timeout and he got up the second I put him there, I sat him back down and sometimes even held him on the couch myself. He got the idea. I even told him if he did not listen and do what his mom and I needed him to do, I would write him up!"

LM: "That's incredible!"

Matthew: "Yeah, he told me he would fire me if I did not listen to him and I don't want to be fired. He told me who I could be the boss of, and it wasn't him or Mom. Sometime I can be the boss of Jody (little brother) when I show him how to do something, but that's it. He told me I was his assistant boss, but assistant bosses had to listen to the big boss. Dad's the big boss."

On one occasion during our last time together, when Matthew wanted to type on my secretary's typewriter, he was told "no" and, while he disliked the answer, went back to playing until his father told him he could go visit with my secretary. Later he gained that privilege since he listened and did as he was told. Matthew was now more careful with his little brother (although the parents are still working on that aspect . . . teaching him to be gentle) and continued to listen to his parents throughout our time together. He seemed more respectful of his parents and they of him. He also appeared happier and much less aggressive. His mom told me she was going to begin helping Matthew learn to ask his classmates what games they wanted to play instead of telling them what he wanted to play each day. While he admitted that was hard, his mom promised to help him learn how to do this by visiting his classroom often at recess and by brainstorming with Matthew daily how to ask his friends what they want to play at school "just for today."

Concluding Comments

"The child is not honored if we always expect him to grow up,
because a child is not grown up."

—*Thomas Moore,* Care of the Soul, *p. 50*

As you read through this chapter, perhaps you noticed something: in each case, the children were not asked "Why are you afraid or upset in elevators," or "Why do you hit your little brother or father," or "Why are you so angry?" Attempts to answer all of these questions had tried and failed not only the family's attempts at helping the child, but in assisting the children to feel worse about themselves. Needless to say, their "problems" continued to influence their lives and the lives of their family members.

The solutions to the problems that were discovered by the children and their parents in this chapter evolved from their own abilities. As you watch your children during the next week, determine the times when you do not allow a "problem" to *interfere* with your family life or come between you and your child. Watch closely for the times when your children do not allow a problem to interfere with their school life, their friends and siblings. Watch for the absence of problems. This is the hardest entity to see, but within them may be the solutions you have been searching for. Your discovery will influence your children and the manner in which they may deal someday with their own children.

> *"You will never really know what kind of parent you were*
> *or if you did it right or wrong. Never. And you will*
> *worry about this and them as long as you live. But when*
> *your children have children and you watch them do what*
> *they do, you will have part of an answer."*

—*Robert Fulghum,* It Was on Fire When I Lay Down on It, *p. 102*

Chapter 5

Finding the Path of Least Resistance

New Maps for Assessing Serious Problems

"Believe that life is worth living and your belief will help create the fact."

—*William James*

M arla, age fourteen, came reluctantly with her mom, a principal in a local high school, to talk to me early one morning. Marla had been stating to her parents that she wanted to kill herself and had made her point one evening by taking over 30 non-aspirin tablets. As Marla became sick, her parents arrived home to find the empty non-aspirin bottles and realized that their daughter was serious about taking her life. After a visit to the emergency room, her parents called a physician who met with Marla for thirty minutes and told her parents that she was "suffering from Bipolar Disorder" (American Psychiatric Association, p. 225). Her parents were perplexed because, until this time, Marla had never had any emotional problems, school problems, or especially mood swings—conditions the physician referred to as now being prominent in her life. Marla's parents were given two pre-scriptions for the disorder, yet they decided to seek a second opinion at another doctor's office before filling them.

Upon their consultation with another physician, the physician commented that their daughter seemed very depressed. He then referred them to me for counseling.

Meeting Marla was challenging at first, since she was not inter-ested in talking about herself. Accompanied by her mother initially, her mom described her daughter as "a teenager who was just going through some typical hard times that all teens go through." I asked Marla if she would like to talk privately and she said "yes." After her mother left the office, Marla began to tell me about the suicidal thoughts that were bothering her to a great degree. She reported that the thoughts haunted her day and night and, while she wished they would go away, nothing she did or her family did seemed to help. When I asked her what the thoughts were like, she said it was a deep, deep depression that took over and kept her very sad.

Noticing how sincere Marla seemed as she described her "depression," I began to talk with her in the following manner.

LM: "I'm so glad to have the chance to talk to you. I have to admit, though, that I am curious about how you have helped your-self to stay alive during the past two weeks since you took the non-aspirin tablets."

Marla: "I really hated how it felt when I got sick. I never want to go through that again. Besides, now my parents watch me like a hawk."

LM: "How does that help?"

Marla: "Well, they are nicer to me, especially my mom, but I still don't think they are taking me seriously about how depressed I am. It's really bad."

LM: "Marla, does the 'depression' you are describing to me occur all of the time?"

Marla: "It seems that way."

LM: "If I were to give you a scale of 1 to 10, with '1' meaning it never bothered you and '10' meaning it bothered you day and night, each minute of the day, in absolutely everything you do, when would you say it is at its worst?"

free of "depression"							*bothered by "depression"*		
1	*2*	*3*	*4*	*5*	*6*	*7*	*8*	*9*	*10*

Marla: "The night I took the pills, that was a 10 for sure. It feels like it's always there."

LM: "This really sounds terrible. I wonder, are there ever times when it's not around so much?"

Marla: "When I'm with my friends it's not as tough."

LM: "Where would you be on the same scale when you are with your friends?"

Marla: "About a 5."

LM: "How does being with your friends move you to a 5?"

Marla: "I feel comfortable with them . . . we talk about other things . . . we make plans to do things . . . fun stuff."

LM: "And tell me, has the 'depression' that you're talking about caused you to miss school, fail classes, lose friends, stop eating, or anything else?"

Marla: "No, actually I'm in Honors' classes so I have to keep my grades up. I'm supposed to be joining the National Honor Society in the spring so I work pretty hard at school."

LM: "That's incredible. With all of this going on, you still study and make really good grades. How exactly do you do that?"

Marla: "I don't know . . . I guess I just always have. It's just that I think that's part of the problem. . . . You see, I want to drop a couple of the Honors' classes in the spring so I can take a break, but my mother wants me to stay in them all year. I get really tired sometimes and I don't have time to go out with my friends because I have so much school work."

LM: "Marla, if a miracle happened tonight while you were asleep and you woke up tomorrow when things were much better, what do you think would be different for you?"

Marla: "My mother would be backing off from pushing me so hard. Maybe we would get along somehow. She would be yelling at me less and show me that she appreciated something about me. Sometimes I think she hates me because I'm not perfect. I would also have some free time for a change."

LM: "Sounds like a really good idea. Tell me, when was the last time you and Mom got along so that you could tell her what you needed from her?"

Marla: "Last year."

LM: "What was different then?"

Marla: "I guess she and I liked to do things together. She's impossible to talk to now . . . you could ask my father . . . all she does is yell."

Creating a New Map . . . from Old Paths

As I did a *solution-focused* "assessment" for "Major Depressive Disorder," which the referring physician had requested, I looked for certain "symptoms," designated by the *Diagnostic and Statistical Manual of Mental Disorders* [DSM, V] (1995). This is a manual utilized by mental health practitioners and psychiatrists to identify various mental disorders. As I assessed the situation that was bothering Marla, I was relieved to hear that there were a **few** times when Marla did not experience feeling "depressed." Additionally, I learned that Marla still had goals for the near future and that she wanted things to be different with her mom. This way of thinking allowed me to talk to Marla more about solutions rather than problems, creating a new map with her.

As this chapter develops, realize that any serious concern you may have with your child or adolescent can be substituted for the dialogue surrounding Marla's "depression." The strategies in this chapter are not specifically tied to "curing" any certain problem; they *are* designed to help you design a better "map" with your child/adolescent. Marla, her parents, and physicians had chosen the "typical" map of looking at what was wrong in Marla's life. As a *problem-focused* map, they found what they were looking for . . . many problems but no solutions. When Marla and her mom began to look for ways around the roadblocks, which they had forgotten were secret passageways, their relationship improved and Marla's "depression" faded. As you read through the typical "symptoms" of Major Depression, think of each description as an attempt to "map" what was wrong with Marla. Then consider Marla's and my dialogue thus far in this chapter and carefully watch for any "exceptions" to these descriptions.

Diagnostic "Symptoms" of Major Depression (DSM, IIIR, pp. 222–223)

- depressed mood (or can be irritable mood in children and adolescents) most of the day, nearly every day

- markedly diminished interest or pleasure in all, or almost all, activities most of the day, nearly every day

- significant weight loss or weight gain when not dieting, or decrease or increase in appetite nearly every day

- insomnia or hypersomnia nearly every day . . . psychomotor agitation or retardation nearly every day

- fatigue or loss of energy nearly every day

- feelings of worthlessness or excessive or inappropriate guilt nearly every day

- diminished ability to think or concentrate, or indecisiveness, nearly every day

- recurrent thoughts of death, recurrent suicidal ideation without a specific plan, or a suicide attempt or a specific plan for committing suicide

As I talked with Marla, I listened for the above criteria only as a preventive measure. She had attempted to harm herself and it was important to consider these "symptoms" in order to be the most helpful and keep her safe. However, as I listened to her, I also heard the following exceptions to a few of the "symptoms" above. At this point, I began to think differently;

instead of Marla having symptoms in her life, I thought of her as having "complaints," and noticed that she did not meet **all** of the criteria described. Instead, she taught me the following "exceptions," which gave us a new destination to talk about:

- she was interested in joining the honor society . . . in the future
- she was not so depressed when she was with or talking to her friends . . . she was happier
- she was motivated to do her school work, although "depressed" and tired . . . she persevered
- she could recall good times with her mother and her enjoyment of them . . . slightly hopeful
- she had fun planning activities with her friends . . . in the future
- she wanted a better relationship with her mother . . . plans for the future

When Does the Problem Not Occur? . . . Discovering New Pathways

When Marla expressed the "exceptions" to the *depression* she initially believed was occurring constantly, she enabled me to be even more helpful to her. The exceptions gave us clues to solutions and taught her that she was not totally stricken by depression and that, in fact, there were times when she was already having what she really wanted. The exceptions also gave me reassurance that Marla had the ability to look into the future with some degree of hopefulness and that she saw herself in that future. While she had recently attempted to kill herself, she told me she did not have a current plan nor did she like the effects of the overdose of the non-aspirin tablets. Because of this desire to not harm herself at the present moment, I focused on her abilities and "exceptions" instead of focusing on figuring out "why" she wanted to take her life.

She also taught me that her family had helped her to stay alive through their watchfulness and their concerns. My concern was that if I had focused only on the symptoms of depression, she might have continued to feel "sick." My desire instead was to help her see that she was "depressed" only sometimes, and while she was slightly reluctant to do this at first, eventually she realized that her goals were acceptable to someone else and that was empowering. As we ended our first hour together:

LM: "I think it's pretty remarkable that, in spite of the awful depression that you describe to me, you continue to do your school work, keep your good friends and even imagine how you want things to be at home with your mom. If you don't mind, I'd like you to do something that would be really helpful to both of us before our next time together. As you go through each day during the next week, would you mind watching for other times when the 'depression' is not so bothersome to you? Maybe you could watch even more for the places you are, who you are with that really makes the depression less of a problem for you."

Talking About Suicide

At this point, I asked to talk to Marla's mom, who promptly told me she knew she was the cause of Marla's troubles. She asked if she should take her daughter's suicidal attempt serious and I told her "yes." There are all sorts of opinions about taking such threats as serious. However, when adolescents harm themselves or say they are going to harm themselves, either jokingly or seriously, I encourage you to *always take them seriously* and check out the situation using the following questions:

- **"Do you have a plan to make yourself dead?"**

  This is an important question. Adolescents too often do not perceive suicide as permanent. They may be upset over the loss of a girlfriend or boyfriend and may want to "show someone" and "make people sorry for the way they treated me." Saying "dead" vs. "hurt yourself" has more impact.

- **"When, how, and where will you make yourself 'dead'?"**

  This question will help you to assess if there is a plan. If an adolescent tells you how he/she might harm himself/herself or, as in Marla's case, takes medications, or finds a knife or gun, carefully watch your offspring.

- **"Who will suffer the most if you make yourself 'dead'? How many people will be hurt by your action of making yourself 'dead'? What might you miss out on for the next few years if you take this action?"**

  Asking this question assists the adolescent in visualizing the family/peer group who is important to him/her. It also allows the adolescent to feel surrounded by people who do care, instead of feeling all alone. Even if the teen can only think of one person, that person knows others who know others and this has an impact on all of their lives.

After you have assessed the situation with the above questions, your next approach needs to be different to achieve different results. Typically, the manner in which parents approach their teen after finding horrific drawings, vulgar music, suicidal notes, obscene language, and death statements on their notebook binders is to confront the adolescent with a furrowed brow and examine their rooms for "evidence," confirming and concretizing that a problem now exists.

New Destinations Require New Maps. Throw Away the Old One . . . You've Already Been There!

This "typical map to dealing with problems" often does little except to infuriate the adolescent, confirm that he/she *is* the problem, and set up roadblocks to family harmony. It is a logical, first-response, instinctive map to follow when you are worried about your child. However, in order to produce a new story with your child, you *must do something different or the behaviors will stay the same.* Many an adolescent and child has told me that they want to listen and hear their parents but their parents are too loud to be heard! To be the most helpful to your offspring, keep your cool and become interested in your adolescents' thoughts instead of accusing them. Consider asking the following questions the next time you become worried or concerned:

"Hmm, this looks really interesting. The drawings are different from those you usually draw. What does this say to you?"

"I notice that your friends are changing. Tell me, what does this crowd do for you that the other crowd did not?"

"Your music is really different now. Tell me what you like about this group?"

"I notice you seem to like more privacy lately. What do you like about being alone?"

"I noticed you have dropped out of athletics. Are there other interests you are finding more interesting?"

You may be surprised to learn of the answers to these questions. You may also find yourself relieved. Nonetheless, you are more likely to open and develop communication between yourself and your adolescent in this nonthreatening way than through confronting them with your worries. As you learn this information from your adolescent, also do yourself one more favor. Begin to ask yourself:

> *"What am I doing, or what is our family doing differently when Joey is <u>not</u> isolating (as depressed, as angry, as uncooperative, as defiant)?"*

And,

> *"When was the last time I felt better about Joey's behavior? What was going on in our family life then? What part did I (or other family members) play that might have made a difference? What would Joey say was different then?"*

Mapmaker, Mapmaker, Make Me a Map!

Marla's mom had recently realized that her boisterous, offensive manner of talking to her daughter was not working. Her husband assured her that her brusque attempts to "snap our daughter out of her depression" made things worse. Her "old map" consisted of the following routes, yet the desired destination was to have a happy, healthy, productive, academically successful and respectful daughter who communicated openly with her family.

The Old Map:

- *If Marla tries to back out of studying, threaten or ground her.*
- *If Marla talks back to me, yell louder.*
- *Always lose my cool with her so she knows who's boss.*
- *Ground her indefinitely and make her study; she is too smart to fail.*

When I asked Marla's mom if her strategies had worked, she said, "Of course not!" I then asked her how she wanted things to be. To her surprise, her goals were the same as Marla's; communicate again, feel less stressed, enjoy each other, and relax. As Marla's mom and I talked, she taught me about some of her abilities which gave me clues as to how she might design a better "new map" to her destination.

LM: "Take me back to a time when you and Marla were able to communicate, have a good relationship, and you were more patient with her."

Mom: "Before she was thirteen. She had always been in Honors' classes and she is so bright. She enjoyed doing well in school. After she entered junior high school and became more popular, things went downhill and her studies went with them. That's when I had to stay on her about her grades and then we really began to clash."

LM: "Tell me about your job at school. There must be times when you feel overwhelmed with all of the teenagers you work with each day, yet, in order to do your job and keep your job, you probably have to stay pretty calm. . ."

Mom: "Daily . . . constantly . . . it's like I have to just use all of this willpower to not explode. I know that keeping my cool is essential."

LM: "Interesting. How do you do that?"

Mom: "I literally take breaks, timeouts, whatever. When a student is brought in by a teacher, I am likely to take a deep breath and then meet with them. I've always had a temper. I don't do well cold turkey. I need some time to get my thoughts together."

LM: "If you were to use this method with Marla, the daughter whom you are wanting to win back into your life, as sort of an experiment during the next week, what might you do?"

Mom: "Probably I would pull up in the garage, sit a few minutes, and then go in the house. Usually I am the worst at the end of the day. That's when her attitude is rough and I play right into it."

LM: "What else?"

Mom: "My husband is really good at pointing out when I get carried away. I could ask him to watch and give me a high sign."

LM: "What else?"

Mom: "I think maybe I just want things to be better."

LM: "I really believe you. I also think that as the professional you are, you would not use the same strategy with the same student over and over if it failed . . . correct?"

Mom: "Of course not."

LM: "What would you think about not using the old strategies and, instead, giving the new ideas that you just described to me a try for a few days? While you do, watch for <u>any</u> different reactions from Marla. Keep a close eye on her responses to you and any changes in behavior that tell you your new strategies are working."

The New Map:

- *Remember, keeping cool is essential. Take deep breaths before talking to Marla.*
- *Take a time out when I am angry. Get my thoughts together. Maybe sit in the car when I come home before going inside.*
- *Ask my husband for a high sign when I begin to "lose it."*
- *Remember just how much I want things to be better. . . I think I'll put a sticky note in my car.*

Marla's mom was not able to meet with Marla during our second session. Instead, her father brought her. He remarked that Marla was showing a vast improvement. She no longer had any suicidal thoughts or remarks and she and her mom were beginning to get along. He remarked that he knew if her mom would only watch her attitude, his daughter would improve. However, his wife's nature was to comment and be too directive. He was pleased that his "strong-willed" wife could show patience again. I wrote Marla's mom a letter that afternoon commending her on her new strategies and complimented her on showing her daughter that a "strong" woman is the strongest when she controls her desire to control others. At our third and last meeting over a year ago, Marla had evolved into a happier, less-stressed young lady who is taking only two Honors' classes (at mom's request). She never took medication.

Give Equal Time to the "Exceptions!"

Marla's reentry into life developed from her identification of the "exceptions" to the descriptions given about Major Depressive Disorder. If Marla had showed more "symptoms" of "depression," was lethargic, hopeless, had suicidal thoughts and a plan, was failing school, isolating, and could not describe anytime when she felt slightly better, I might have suggested that she revisit her physician for medication to assist her to physically feel better, but only if that was acceptable to her. It has been my experience that people (especially children and adolescents) are more likely to follow through with a new plan (or map) when they are the mapmakers. The key is learning how to write the map together so you all know where to go. Page 00 contains a "problem inventory to review before your family attempts the next activity entitled "M.A.P.S." *(Mapping A Problem's Solution)*, suggested by a friend and colleague, Stephen Chilton, M.S.

M.A.P.S.
A Family Activity
(developed collaboratively with Stephen Chilton, M.S.)

The purpose of this activity is to join together as a family (parents and siblings) in a family "meeting" and talk about the current "map" that has created a problem. This is a different way of looking at things; instead of coming together to discuss a problem family member, *everyone* comes together to discuss their roles in creating the current "map." Then, by brainstorming and identifying everyone's current role in creating the problem, the *chief mapmaker* can ask everyone for new roles, thereby creating a new "map," where old problem *destinations* cannot exist.

You will need the following materials:

- large sheets of construction paper (one piece for each family member)
- crayons, markers or pencils for each family member
- 3 × 5 index cards
- basket or shoebox or bowl
- self-sticking notepads for each family member

Gathering New Thoughts About the Problem

Complete Before the M.A.P.S. Activity

1. Describe below the "problem" that seems to be troubling your child/adolescent. Ask yourself how your child/adolescent typically handled problems in the past. (What is his/her typical "map"?) What are your child/adolescent's typical strengths and abilities?

2. What time of day, which hours in the day, and in which situations and interactions with others does the problem seem to be less of a problem to your child/adolescent? (When do some of the "symptoms" disappear?) What are you or others doing that seems to help during that time?

3. Does your son/daughter talk about plans in the near future (such as tomorrow, the dance next week, summer vacation, a job)? Has your son/daughter continued a social life? How is school progressing? Consider any "yes" answers to these questions "exceptions" and write them below.

4. Ask your child/adolescent to take you back to a time when just a little of that wish occurred for him/her in another situation, time, and place. Begin to ask him/her how they helped those desired situations to occur. Ask what you did then and could do now to recreate that time as well. Recall times when you helped your child/adolescent through other smaller problems. What seemed to help?

Directions

1. Choose a *chief mapmaker.* A parent is the most appropriate person for this role. He/she needs to assess the strengths and abilities of all family members before the exercise begins by reviewing the questions on the page entitled "Gathering New Thoughts About the Problem." As the exercise begins, the chief mapmaker says:

   "We are here because we are bothered by a problem. The problem is not any one person in this room. What we are going to do for a few minutes today is to think about how our family life is going right now, with the problem being in charge. We are going to call it "the problem map" or the plans we have used in the past to get where we are now."

   The chief mapmaker then takes a piece of paper and draws the problem for all to see. For example:

   "Anger is a problem that is really bothering me. I notice that it starts bothering Alex, your fifteen-year-old brother, and then it moves through our family. (Drawing) Then, I let it bother me because I scream back at Alex, then I get upset with Angie, and Angie pouts. Then, Dad gets upset because we are all upset and grounds Alex. Sometimes the problem then makes Alex sneak out at night and Dad becomes very worried and tired and then Dad gets irritable the next day with everyone. This is how "The Anger Problem" has put up roadblocks in our lives. Dad is tired of its control over all of us and Dad is sure all of you are just as tired of it too."

   "As your chief mapmaker, I've been watching you all week. I decided that in order to make a new map with all of you today, I needed to figure out what you were all good at so we could really put up a fight toward the anger problem. I noticed the following ..." (The chief mapmaker now reads the attributes of the family members to each of them and asks for ideas from the family about what he/she (chief) does okay.

2. The chief mapmaker now looks at each family member and describes strengths and abilities that were noticed during the week and during *all the years of his/her time in the family.* For example, he/she may say to fifteen-year-old Alex:

   "Alex, for fourteen and a half years, you have been the most respectful, fun-loving and kind son any mom could ever hope for. You are smart, helpful at times and I can always depend on you to give me a really good argument when you really believe in something."

   To Dad:

   "John, you care so much about keeping our family together. You work hard for us and when you make quick decisions to keep the anger out, I know you mean well. You are a patient boss and your employees have always respected your calm manner and kind spirit."

3. The chief mapmaker now passes out 3 × 5 cards to each family member. Each member is given a card for each member of the family. (For example, four family members = four cards per person.) The chief asks each person to look at the family members and (a) remember times when they really got along and (b) write something they like about each of their family members. All of the cards are put in a basket in front of the chief mapmaker who then reads all of the cards to the family. Keep the authors anonymous for fun.

4. The family members are now asked to draw a new map, or "dream map," using their family's assets so the anger problem does not bother them so much. If a family member begins to say things such as "You just need to stop Alex from fighting with me," reply:

   "I agree. On our old map, when Alex fought, we all did things that kept the anger around. Today, we're going to think how we can all make a new map so the anger doesn't have a chance. Alex, how would you like things to be?"

This may mean drawing pictures of each family member and connecting each member with a line that has a suggestion written on it. This can become the "dream map." The chief mapmaker will help the members turn their complaints into suggestions by using the following guiding questions:

Complaint	Solution Reply
"He needs to stop hitting me when he wants something from my room that I am using..."	*"Instead of hitting you, what do you want him to do instead so you can cooperate?"*
"Get Dad to stop yelling at me before he even knows what's going on. I get blamed for everything!"	*"What would you see your dad doing instead when he gets upset with you that tells you he is listening first?"*
"Mom, you take out your anger with me. You get so mad at Alex that you don't have time to be nice to me like you used to."	*"So what would you like to see me doing with you again that would tell you I was less angry and had more time for you?"*

Can you see the difference between the two columns? The "complaints" are listened to, yet they are changed into questions that give solutions for change. This question encourages responsibility on the part of the complainer and, since you accept the complaint, lessens resistance and changes your relationship on the spot! The simple formula is: *"Okay, what would you like to see instead?"*

5. Finally, each family member shows and explains his/her new dream map. The chief mapmaker makes sure that the family member explains the "new connections" and also tells how he/she will help the connections to happen just for a week. At the end of this exercise, a combined map is made and placed strategically in the house where everyone can see the progress of reaching their destination.

6. Each family member is given a small self-sticking notepad and is asked to write notes to those family members during the week who are sticking to the new map and not letting the old map rule them. Let everyone put their notes on the map near the person's drawing. For very young children, I suggest that parents ask to see the notes first, to keep them oriented toward compliments.

To review the process, the steps are:

a. Say in your kindest manner that your family is being bothered by a problem.

b. Mention that this problem is not a person. Then explain how the "problem" seems to move through your family.

c. Invite them to draw with you a new map to fight the problem.

d. Express to each person his/her abilities and assets you discovered.

e. Each person draws a "dream map."

f. Together, the family constructs one dream map with every member on it. Notes are placed on the map to give compliments and gauge how the progress is going.

How is this interaction different from a typical confrontation about, for example, an anger problem, running away, depression, etc.? For one thing, the activity produces solutions, suggestions, different ways of seeing other family members, lessens blame, promotes new perceptions, encourages others to see their actions as influencing others, and teaches everyone that there have been times when the problem did not exist.

In the Case of Divorce . . .
Gaining Assistance from the Other Parent

In stepfamilies, where children might visit the other parent on the weekend, ask the other parent if he/she would be interested in knowing what you are doing in your family so he/she can **also** have influence over the problem in their son/daughter's life. It is more helpful to explain *first* how **you** are discovering your role in the life of the problem, how siblings are discovering their roles, and how what you are discovering is beginning to work with your son/daughter. This is a more nonthreatening manner of asking for cooperation. Pages 126 and 127 are sheets to give to your child's parent/stepparent and below is a sample of how to ask for help:

> *"I know you have been worried about Paul as much as I have. Would you mind, over the weekend, watching for times when he is not so angry, when Susie and Jean do not fight with him, and what you might do that helps them all to stay calm? All of us would really appreciate your observations. If you write a love note for each of the kids, I would be glad to give the notes to them later."*

"When Is the Problem Absent?"

Helpful Observations from Divorced Parents and Stepparents

1. *Below, please list times, activities, situations, interactions in which the problem was not bothering _____:*

    _____

    _____

    _____

2. *Name and describe the strengths of your children below, recalling all of the years of their life, their favorite activities, sports, interests, and what you have always loved about them. (Please share this information with them before the weekend is over!)*

    _____

    _____

    _____

    _____

3. *Which strategies have you tried or noticed that seem to work with _____ that help control the problem?*

    _____

    _____

    _____

    _____

A Love Note

To: _____

From: _____

_____

_____

_____

_____

parent signature

· ·

A Love Note

To: _____

From: _____

_____

_____

_____

_____

parent signature

What If No One Cooperates?

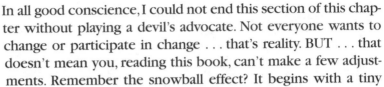

In all good conscience, I could not end this section of this chapter without playing a devil's advocate. Not everyone wants to change or participate in change . . . that's reality. BUT . . . that doesn't mean you, reading this book, can't make a few adjustments. Remember the snowball effect? It begins with a tiny snowball and grows larger and larger. As you examine the "problem" that is bothering your child/adolescent, and as you examine your actions around the problem, remember, if you do anything different at all, you will contribute to change.

For example, June, a 55-year-old mom came to see me several months ago about her 24-year-old daughter, Lisa, herself a mom of a one-year-old son. June was upset because Lisa demanded that she (June) baby-sit the toddler practically every weekend, all day. At times during the week, too, Lisa would invite herself and her husband to dinner at June's home. Whenever June would try and assert herself with replies such as, "I can't baby-sit tonight, I'm too tired," Lisa would become hysterical and accuse her mom of not caring about her grandson. Other times, Lisa would call June and consult with her on every decision regarding the baby, money, jobs, etc. June attempted to give Lisa advice, but Lisa would argue that June didn't know what she was talking about. June would then become angry and come across—in her words—as a "witch." At one point, Lisa threatened to never let June see her grandson again.

As June and I talked, I learned that she had worked in the same company for ten years in employee services. I asked her how she might treat a fellow employee who was taking her for granted. She smiled and said, "Wow, does that ever happen to me. I often have to just take them aside and say, 'Look, I know you need me to do this paper work for you but I can't today. Catch me some other time.' Usually they stop. I just don't like people mad at me."

June told me she was also very worried about her daughter's marriage. She mentioned that her daughter seemed too dependent on her and not dependent on her husband.

LM: "If I gave you a scale of 1 to 10, with '1' meaning you never gave in the relationship with your daughter, Lisa, and '10' meaning you have given everything, where would you say you are?"

June: "I would say a 9."

LM: "Same scale, where would you say Lisa is?"

June: "Probably about a 3."

	Lisa						June		
	x						x	
1	2	3	4	5	6	7	8	9	10

As we both smiled, I commented that she was definitely ahead of her responsibilities with Lisa. Jokingly, she looked down and said, "Too ahead, right?" I asked June to think about the way she was able to deal with the employees at work who attempted to take advantage of her and invited her to think about doing something similar with Lisa just during the next week, taking caution to remain the kind, caring mom she had been restraining herself from being. Since Lisa had refused to come to counseling with her mom, it was up to June.

Two weeks later, June came back to see me, smiling and relaxed. "It worked. I can't believe it actually worked!" According to June, during the last two weeks, whenever Lisa called or dropped by with the baby, and June could not accommodate her, June hugged her daughter and apologized for not having the time but promised to do it soon. She told Lisa she would be in touch the next day to plan a time to care for her grandson. Thereafter, whenever Lisa called June for advice, she told her she did not know what her daughter should do . . . and then she kindly suggested she talk to her husband. Within two weeks, June was happier, Lisa was beginning to depend more on her husband, and June kept the baby on her time.

This case is important because it shows what parents, couples, individuals, and employers have proven to me over and over: when one person changes, someone else has to change. This does not mean that the other person will change voluntarily or easily; in fact, the other person will often dig in his/her heels and swear off any type of change on his/her part. Eventually, when the "map" changes, a new one has to be created. The important step: "Doing something different can and will make a difference."

Additional Assessment/Exception Tools for Serious Situations

The remainder of this chapter is designed as a working tool to assess the following "most-asked-about" situations of concern to parents:

- ADD (Attention Deficit Disorder)
- Oppositional Defiant Disorder
- Major Depressive Disorder

To give you the most information, I am including for each "situation of concern," diagnostic tools from the *Diagnostic and Statistical Manual of Mental Disorders III R,* so that you may see where your son/daughter is in reference to "symptoms." More important, I am including an "Exceptions to the Problem" sheet so you may begin to use a solution-focused approach in each situation to reassure yourself and begin to influence your son/daughter's well-being.

Attention Deficit Disorder Symptoms (DSM, IIIR, pp. 52–53)

- often fidgets with hands or feet or squirms in seat (in adolescents, may be limited to subjective feelings of restlessness)
- has difficulty remaining seated when required to do so
- is easily distracted by extraneous stimuli
- has difficulty awaiting turn in games or group situations
- often blurts out answers to questions before they have been completed
- has difficulty following through on instructions from others (not due to oppositional behavior or failure of comprehension); e.g., fails to finish chores
- has difficulty sustaining attention in tasks or play activities
- often shifts from one uncompleted activity to another
- has difficulty playing quietly
- often talks excessively
- often interrupts or intrudes on others; e.g., butts into other children's games
- often does not seem to listen to what is being said to him or her
- often loses things necessary for tasks and activities at school or at home (pens, pencils, books, toys, assignments)
- often engages in physically dangerous activities without considering possible consequences (not for the purpose of thrill-seeking); e.g., runs into street without looking

Looking for Exceptions
with Energetic Kids

Home Life:

1. *If you followed around your child/adolescent each day this week, 24 hours a day, in what places, situations, or with whom would you find him/her paying attention and behaving slightly better? What seems to work in these situations,* **slightly?** *Ask your child/adolescent for this information.*

   _____

   _____

   _____

2. *If you were to watch your child today very closely and notice the times when he/she stays on task for a few minutes longer, would he/she require your constant reminders, or would he/she need a note taped to the bedroom door to remind him/her of one thing to do? WATCH! What seems to work with your child/adolescent, according to him/her?*

   _____

   _____

   _____

   _____

3. *In your family, which parent is successful at encouraging your child to complete a task more efficiently? What does he/she do that seems to work? Ask your child/adolescent what seems to make the difference.*

   _____

   _____

   _____

Social Life:

4. *As you glance back over the years, were there times when he/she paid attention better and had few to no behavior problems? What was happening then at home, with friends, or school that made things easier? What would your child/adolescent say?* _____

_____

_____

5. *In which situations does your child get along socially? Does he/she play better one on one or in a group of many or a few children/adolescents? Write these down and ask your child/adolescent which is easier/better for him/her.*

_____

_____

School Life:

6. *Recall times during your child's school career when he/she did well in school behaviorally and/or academically. What was different during that time? What were his/her teachers like, friends, routine? What did you do that helped? List the school year, the teachers and, together with your child/adolescent, talk about what you both think seemed to make a difference so that school was successful.* _____

_____

_____

_____

7. *Which school subjects does your child/adolescent do well at? List them below. Besides each subject, ask your child/adolescent what the teacher does that keeps his/her interest. Where does he/she sit in the classroom that seems to work? Ask your child/adolescent what the teacher (and the subject!) does for him/her* **personally** *that makes school fun and interesting. The answers will tell you how he/she learns best.* _____

_____

_____

Conclusive Ideas for ADHD Kids and Parents

Our son Ryan, age 12, was diagnosed as being bothered by ADHD (Attention Deficit Hyperactivity Disorder) seven years ago and takes 20mg of Ritalin®, daily. Ritalin® is a prescription medication that is sometimes helpful to ADHD children/adolescents. While his behavior is often frustrating to our family, his delightful abilities have taught us that *we* must accommodate his differences as he accommodates *ours!*

I have learned that in order to help Ryan with homework, he:

- *needs to sit no longer than 30 minutes at a time*
- *must be checked on and encouraged every 10 to 15 minutes (this is increasing)*
- *needs reassurance because he is easily frustrated with too many papers*
- *must have complete quiet and no distractions to concentrate*

I remember once, several years ago, how he brought home a paper from school with a grade of 50. His teacher had allowed him to take it home and finish it when he became very upset with himself. When he showed me the paper I *assumed* he needed my help. As I went into his room (which had the door closed) to help him ten minutes later, he presented to me a completed paper with all of the answers correct! When I asked him how he did it so quickly, he told me, "Mom, I just needed things to be quiet. That's all I needed." Enough said; listen and learn. Your child/adolescent will teach you all you need to know; look at them with fascination and take *your* vitamins!

If your child/adolescent seems to be bothered by ADHD, please realize that many ADHD kids are very bright. They are often very artistic and extremely creative. Our job is to find and create an environment at home and school in which they can be themselves, yet curtail their "energy" at appropriate times. This can be an overwhelming task.

Medically, today, we know that neurologically the brain of an ADHD person is slightly different from that of a non-ADHD person. Since it works so differently, the person must learn to adapt his/her behavior differently. Often your child/adolescent will have the best suggestions for doing this. Ask: *"How would you like things to be in class?" "What would you suggest doing just for today so the teacher notices the neat kid you are/gets off your back, etc.?"*

If your son or daughter fits some of the criteria for ADHD, consider modifying your behavior *first* to see if changes in the environment can assist him/her. Visit the classroom at school and check with your son/daughter's teachers and find out what might go on in school that makes a difference. As you learn how to assist your *energetic* child, pass along your discoveries to his/her teacher. In Chapter 6, you will find additional ways of contacting schools and asking for their assistance, effectively.)

Allow the information from the "exception" worksheets to give you clues to solutions with your child/adolescent. The symptoms merely "diagnose." The "exceptions" can tell you and your child how success can happen once again.

Oppositional Defiant Disorder Symptoms (DSM, III R, p. 57)

- often loses temper
- often argues with adults
- often actively defies or refuses adult requests or rules; e.g., refuses to do chores at home
- often deliberately does things that annoy other people; e.g., grabs other children's hats
- often blames others for his or her own mistakes
- is often touchy or easily annoyed by others
- is often angry and resentful
- is often spiteful or vindictive
- often swears or uses obscene language

Looking for Exceptions with Challenging Oppositional Kids

Home Life:

1. *Glance back to the past and recall times when your child/adolescent was more receptive of talking to you and doing things you asked him/her to do. What was different then at home, with friends, or in the way you talked and related to him/her? Ask your child/adolescent during a quiet time this week, when it is convenient to him/her what was different then.*

   _____

   _____

   _____

2. *As you go through this week, watch for times when your child/adolescent does not seem so angry or easily frustrated. In what situations does he/she seem happier and **slightly** more cooperative? Who is there and what is different in any way? When you notice even the **smallest** bit of compliance, say: "I really appreciate your help/listening/answering me . . . even though you have a lot to do, you took the time to do it. I'm impressed."*

   _____

   _____

   _____

When you "catch" your child/adolescent slightly cooperative, write what impressed you the most on a note like the one below and leave it somewhere for him/her to find.

NOTICE
I noticed you!

_____

_____

_____

135

Social Life:

3. *How would your child/adolescent describe how you feel about his/her friends? When was the last time you invited them to your house? If the friends have changed for the worse, how in the past have you talked to your child/adolescent in a way that he/she heard your concerns? What would he/she say would help when you talk?*

_____

_____

_____

_____

School Life:

4. *Consider all of your child/adolescent's teachers this year and last year. In which classes was your child/adolescent able to maintain an average to above-average conduct grade? What was the teacher like in each of those classes? What would your child/adolescent say the teacher did that lessened his/her anger and frustration in class? What discipline methods, if any, worked? Ask!*

_____

_____

_____

_____

5. *Looking at the classes in question 4, ask your child/adolescent "what was it about this class" (regarding the subject) that helped you to pay attention? From the answers, consider the possibility of your child/adolescent's learning style being very important to his/her behavior. Ask how he/she learns best, specifically!*

_____

_____

_____

_____

Conclusive Ideas for Parents Whose Kids Are Challenging

Having taught junior high school for eight years, I learned first-hand from adolescents that frustration and anger are often closely tied with feeling incompetent. As you complete the "exceptions" worksheet for oppositional kids, consider *not* thinking of your child/adolescent as difficult, defiant, irresponsible or angry, but *instead* as coping with his/her world the best he/she can. As adults, we have 20 to 30 years of experience in the world that adolescents do not. The important task for us is to give this knowledge to our children and adolescents in a way that they will hear us. That's the tricky part! They will *not* hear it through a lecture or criticism. The nature of adolescence is to figure out who one is.

Several times a week I have very angry adolescents come into my office proclaiming that they will never listen to another parent or teacher tell them how bad they are. My task is to first jump on their side by saying:

> *"This sounds horrible. They have no idea who you really are, do they?"*

> *"What do you think it might take to get all of them off your back so you can have some freedom back?"*

At this point I get their attention, they gain validation of how they are feeling, and, together, we are more likely to find a plan to *get their freedom back*. Notice that the goal is *not* "To please the teacher and your parent." No way! Adolescents are, by development, very self-centered. When we cooperate with this self-centeredness, we are more likely to work out plans that assist all of us. Remember, cooperation breeds cooperation.

Major Depressive Disorder

The symptoms were previously listed in this chapter on page 113.

Conclusive Ideas for Parents Who Worry About Their Kids' Happiness

Kids become sad over many things. We can describe it as depression, sadness, isolation, an overwhelming need for privacy, but it is really a normal part of life. Kids also become happy quickly when situations change. When I taught eighth graders in the 1980s I was always surprised how upset they could be in the morning at 8:30 A.M. and how happy they would be by 3:30 P.M.

While many teens become depressed, the important thing to remember is what they really need from you is your support and an environment similar to the times when they were not depressed. Their memories are also short, and their perception of life getting better in the near future seems gloomy. For this reason, asking the questions suggested in the "exceptions" worksheet focuses more on when life was better. A young man, age 19, told me recently that he knew he was depressed because he felt so bored when he sat in the evening with nothing to do. I then asked him: *"When you become 'bored' like that, what do you do to stop being bored?"* He said: *"I usually get up and do something."*

According to DSMI, III R criteria, his ability to get up and do something, motivating himself to be productive, does not indicate depression, even though he used the word to describe the situation. As we ended our session together, I asked him to keep on noticing other ways he fights the "boredom," and even how he might fight it someday when he decided to stay seated!

Concluding Comments

"Treat people as if they were what they should be, and you help them become what they are capable of becoming."

—*Johann Wolfgang von Goethe*

In this chapter I have attempted to give information that will help you to identify the "exceptions" to your child/adolescent's problem. The M.A.P.S. activity was included because of my belief that families are systems. Think of how you react to the *other* systems in your life. Most of us act and react differently at work than we do at home. When things change at work, we react differently again. Changing the system at home can result in changed behaviors.

Additionally, it is very easy to go looking for symptoms; they are sure to pop up when we seek them and even when we do not look for them. The more difficult task is to look for *when the symptoms are not present.* However, it is within those times that you may learn what is occurring for the problem to disappear. These times can bring you reassurance and specific strategies to create more of those problem-free moments

Looking for Exceptions
with Kids Who Become Sad

Home Life:

1. *During the next few days, watch for times when your son/daughter is not so sad or "depressed." Look for the situations in which they seem to smile, become more talkative, and are more part of the family. What happens during those times?* _____

   _____

   _____

2. *Mention to your child/adolescent that you have noticed a sort of "sadness" seems to be bothering them lately. (Check out if this word is okay, or, ask for another word to use that fits the problem.) Ask him/her, with lots of curiosity, "How are you able to cope each day ... go to school, talk to friends ... when the sadness tries to bring you down?" Show them the scale below and ask how big the sadness gets sometimes and how small. Ask what goes on at home sometimes to make it smaller.*

   small   big

   1   2   3   4   5   6   7   8   9   10

   _____

   _____

   _____

Social Life:

3. *Ask your child/adolescent for times in the past when the "sadness" bothered him/her less. Perhaps there were different friends then or activities that seemed to make a difference. Reminisce with your child through looking at photo albums or suggest through remembering the times when you remember him/her being happier.* _____

   _____

   _____

139

4. *Ask your child/adolescent to imagine with you for a moment what a miracle might look like if he/she woke up tomorrow morning and things were better for **him**/**her**. Remember to smile and say, "Be realistic, okay?"*

_____

_____

_____

School Life:

5. *Ask your child/adolescent if there are times when the "sadness" **does not** bother him/her at school. Which classes, which teachers seem to help the sadness shrink? Ask your child how he/she manages to continue to go to school, participate in activities (if any) while the sadness is around.*

_____

_____

_____

6. *As you end your conversation with your child/adolescent, jot down some notes from your conversation and compose a letter to him/her, mentioning how impressed you are that, in spite of the sadness that is bothering him/her, he/she still talked to you about it (even if briefly). Mention the abilities you have always seen in him/her and express confidence that you are there to do whatever is necessary to help him/her shrink the sadness. Sign the letter and leave it in an obvious place for him/her to find.*

_____

_____

_____

Chapter
6

School Problems: You Can Influence the Outcome

"The Wright brothers flew right through the smoke screen of impossibility."

—*Charles Franklin Kettering*

School problems can be bewildering and frightening. The problems are usually dealt with when teachers become concerned about students, call the student's parents, and gather everyone together to hear about the problems bothering "Jimmy." The meeting often ends with parents feeling as if they have failed, the teachers waiting for the parents to *do something* about Jimmy—and all of this occurs while Jimmy is sitting in a classroom somewhere wondering what everyone is saying about him.

Sound familiar? This typical method of *helping* kids succeed is used often today, resulting in arguments, hurt feelings, frustration, and defensiveness. Schools wait for parents to do something, parents blame the school for not doing enough. The worst part is that Jimmy feels so much pressure that he sometimes gives up, drops out, or decides he's dumb.

This chapter is full of true cases of *problem school situations* in which I had the opportunity to intervene or to observe very exceptional teachers work within. As you read them, observe closely for the *differences* in perception that using this solution-focused approach can produce in *everyone* involved.

Story #1: Alternative School or Bust!

The day Jose returned to the middle school in a South Texas town, the teachers and students were ready for him. Jose, a gang member and frequent visitor of the district's alternative program, galloped down the hallway to his drama class where he was to meet Terry, a student teacher, teaching a lesson about puppet making. As Jose entered the class with attitude in hand, Terry greeted him as the rest of the class snickered. Terry continued his lesson as Jose began to irritate the class by being disrespectful to his teacher and walking around the room. At first, Terry tried quieting him down, encouraging him to work and, finally, telling him he might have to visit the vice principal if he did not settle down. Jose seemed to want to keep his reputation in tact. He continued to misbehave and be more disrespectful to Terry. As a last resort, Terry sent Jose to the front office for a discipline slip. As Jose sauntered out of the class as if victorious, Terry hoped that (a) he would make it to the office and (b) that his return would be more pleasant.

Jose re-entered the classroom after ten minutes . . . with the discipline slip chewed up in his mouth. He walked over to Terry in front of the class and spat out the discipline slip onto Terry's shoe. Thinking quickly on his "feet," Terry knew his class was watching for his next move. He also knew Jose's reputation and how Jose was waiting to hear the words "leave my classroom now." Terry also knew this had been tried so often, according to the teachers in his school, that Jose always spent his days in either suspension or in alternative school. To do something risky yet different seemed necessary. Terry said to Jose:

> *"You know, I don't seem to be able to read this pass. Could you maybe smooth it out for me, or possibly go get me another one that I can read?"*

Stunned, Jose smiled, snickered, and then his smile faded as Terry continued the lesson in front of a shocked class. Jose picked up the pieces, sauntered out of the classroom once again, looked back longingly, and returned ten minutes later with a new discipline pass in his hand. He placed the pass on Terry's desk and walked somberly over to his desk where he put his head down. As the class continued, Terry thanked Jose for the new pass and intermittently throughout the class that day walked over to Jose and complimented him on anything he noticed Jose doing, even if minute. As the class ended, Terry watched Jose watch him as he left the classroom.

The next morning, Terry arrived at school at 7:30 A.M. for a faculty meeting. He went to his classroom for a few minutes to get his lesson plan ready and Jose knocked on the open door.

"Mr. Cross, I just wanted to say . . . uh . . . that . . . uh . . . I'm real sorry about yesterday."

Shocked himself, Terry shook his hand and said:

"Hey, well, I appreciate that. I'm glad to have you in my class."

As they talked for a few minutes, Terry saw a side of Jose that many people had probably failed to see; a side that needed attention, validation and some insecurities that needed reinforcement. Throughout the rest of the semester, Terry constantly gave Jose attention. In fact, in the hallways, whenever he saw Jose, Terry did a "high five" with Jose. Jose began to pay attention in Terry's class and was academically successful for most of the semester.

Towards the end of April, a fight broke out between two boys in the back of the room in Terry's class. Terry noticed that Jose got up quickly to participate, then stopped, turned around and sat down in his seat. Terry knew what an enormous change that was for Jose. That afternoon he composed a letter on official school stationery and placed it in an official school envelope. The letter he wrote is similar to the one shown on page 144:

Jose looked at the envelope being placed on his desk the next morning and balked. As he opened the letter and read it, Terry told me later that the smile on his face was worth all the efforts of that semester to find positives in Jose. After reading the letter, Jose looked at Terry and said, "I can take this home and I'm not going to get hit for this one."

Dear Jose,

Today I saw something remarkable in my classroom. I saw you get up to participate in a fight and then I saw you back away. As I watched you, I thought about how much courage it took for you to stop yourself from getting involved. I'm not sure how you did that but I do know I was very impressed with you today. I'm proud to be your teacher.

Signed,

Mr. Cross

Story #2: The Day the Temper Tantrum Met Its Match

Trudy, age 24, a new teacher, had enjoyed her kindergarten class very much during the past year. Things had gone smoothly until a day in April when Bryan arrived. Clad in a "Teenage Mutant Ninja Turtle" T-shirt, Bryan made a grand entrance to the reading center by shoving several students out of his way and sat down in front of the book-shelf. As Trudy approached him, she was met by Bryan's mother, Joann, who was standing in the back of the classroom. Joann was concerned about Bryan's tendency to have temper tantrums and become bossy when he did not get his way. She said it had been a problem in his preschool class and it was still a problem at home. Concerned about making Bryan feel comfortable in class, Trudy asked his mom for any tips on managing Bryan. Joann simply said that he loved the "Teenage Mutant Ninja Turtles," and sometimes in order to get his attention she grounded him for short amounts of time from playing with his Ninja Turtles. While that often got Bryan's attention, within minutes Bryan was back to his misbehavior.

As Trudy watched Bryan, she noticed he was a very bright student. He seemed to be friendly toward the other children as long as they listened to him. He seemed to love the attention from others and when Trudy asked him to help pass out crayons and paper, he was in his element . . . until the tantrum struck.

Around 10:30 the following morning, Bryan became argumentative with another student, hit him, and grabbed all of the student's art supplies, complaining that the student would not share with him. Bryan flung himself on the floor and screamed, pounding the floor with all of his might. Trudy tried to comfort Bryan, but he would not stop. Finally the school counselor was called and sat in the room with Bryan, talking to him for over an hour. By 11:30, when class ended, Trudy was shaken and upset. The tantrums continued for the next two weeks.

The counselor was exhausted and perplexed by Bryan. A parent conference confirmed that these behaviors were nothing new. Bryan simply lost control at times and could not be consoled. His grades were outstanding and his conduct outside of the tantrums had changed for the better. Trudy had modified much of Bryan's behavior by complimenting him when he completed his work quietly. She moved him to the front of the room and gave him ample one-on-one attention. What remained was the issue of controlling the tantrums . . . for Bryan's sake.

That evening, Trudy began to think "how can I cooperate with this student?" She began to mentally list the "exceptions":

- She noticed that he liked the attention she always gave him in class.

- She knew he enjoyed being noticed by the other students and helping her pass out supplies.

- She remembered how he loved playing "Teenage Mutant Ninja Turtles" on the playground with several boys and how he was always the leader.

- Her attempts and the counselor's attempts to talk him out of the tantrums had not worked.

The counselor had referred Bryan for psychological tests with the school psychologist. The tests came back with a normal profile . . . and additional information that he was "strong willed." This was obvious. Something different had to be attempted.

The next morning, Trudy was ready. School began at 8:30 A.M. At 9:00 Bryan was sitting quietly at his desk, doing his work. She walked over to him and whispered:

Trudy: "Bryan, I can hardly believe this. Do you know you have been sitting here for 30 minutes and the 'tantrum' that bothered **you** yesterday is not here? How are you doing this?"

Bryan: "I don't know what you are talking about."

Trudy: "The tantrum . . . the one that bothered you yesterday . . . you have kept it out of our classroom for 30 minutes. You are **very, very strong.**"

Bryan: "I **am** strong."

Trudy: "What would you say about keeping it away from you for the next 30 minutes?" (She showed him the clock at this point.)

Bryan: "Okay." (Looking quite proud of himself)

After thirty minutes had passed, Trudy approached Bryan again.

Trudy: "Oh, my gosh . . . an hour . . . 60 minutes . . . 360 seconds are gone and you have been **totally in control of the tantrum that bothered you yesterday.** You are absolutely the strongest boy I have ever had in kindergarten class! How are you doing this?"

Bryan: "I am, I am really strong. I just decided to not let it bother me today."

Trudy: "Well, you are incredible. Tell me, let's look at the clock together. How long do you want to shoot for now?"

Bryan: "All morning."

Trudy: "What? You can't be serious . . . that's two more hours! How will you do that?"

Bryan: "I'm just going to control it."

Trudy: "Like Raphael does?"

Bryan: "You know who Raphael is?"

Trudy: "Of course. He's the strong turtle, like you."

Staring at his teacher in disbelief, Bryan looked quite puzzled at her knowledge of Raphael, one of the "Teenage Mutant Ninja Turtles." He smiled at her and she told him she would come around for the next two hours and check on "Raphael." By 11:30, Bryan had "kicked the tantrum," according to him, and Trudy allowed him to lead the class to the bus stop. She continued this strategy of setting up the opportunity for *exceptions* to occur for the remainder of the school year. The tantrums disappeared. Trudy's strategy required that she keep a close eye on Bryan, but she noticed that she eventually could go for longer intervals without having to remind him. The change in Bryan's behavior changed the class environment and Bryan became more popular with his classmates. His mother called one day to talk to Trudy about the changes she was seeing at home. Bryan was becoming more polite to his little brother and would, at times, declare how strong he was when his mother asked him to do a chore.

A New Approach for Old Problems

What did these two remarkable teachers do with the information they were given regarding the symptoms and negative behavior of their students?

- They decided to try something different.
- They redescribed the students mentally to themselves, lessening their defensiveness against the students *immediately*.
- They watched carefully for any exceptions to the students' misbehaviors and said something when they noticed them, *directly to the student*.
- They encouraged the exceptions to occur more often by setting up opportunities for the exceptions to occur.
- They acknowledged and became respectful towards the student, even when the student was not respecting the teacher.
- They saw the problems as separate from the students.
- They found ways to cooperate with who the students were . . . and used that strategy to change their behaviors instead of changing the students.

The two stories mentioned are typical of student behaviors *worldwide*. From Prince George, British Columbia, to Sydney, Australia, I have heard the same scenarios and complaints from teachers and counselors who desperately have tried to find ways to change student behaviors. What is *not the same* is the way Terry and Trudy handled the problems that were *bothering* their students. As a former junior high teacher, I remember being taught to look for deficits and change the student's behavior through behavioral modification techniques. Maybe in 1970 those techniques worked, but today, those techniques work with 30 percent or less of the population of students, and those students are usually the ones who seldom misbehave!

Instead of trying to mold Bryan into a student who could control himself or change Jose into a student who respected his teacher, these students changed *their own behavior* because of their teacher's approach to them. A student such as Jose can be found placed in alternative schools over and over and over again. Is this approach working? Apparently not. Yet we continue to suspend him. Sure, his actions disrupt the classroom and some students threaten the classroom and the teachers. Yet, walking through inner city schools (such as Jose's) as a student teacher supervisor, I notice often that *not all teachers have problems* with students, and that *the same teachers do have problems year after year.* What makes the difference? It is how respectfully the successful teachers treat their students *even in the midst of conflict.* Even more important, the teachers who respect their students *rarely have conflict!* Terry and Trudy did not go home in the evenings and think: "Until he changes there is nothing I can do." Or, "He can't function in a normal class setting," or "It must be his homelife," or "His parents will have to straighten him out," or "He needs placement." Instead, they asked themselves:

- How can I cooperate with this student's needs and personality so I can assist him in changing his behavior?
- What can I do differently from what others have done so this student does not respond the same?
- When are the times the behavior does not occur?
- What has been tried before and did not work?
- What might I be doing that is encouraging the problem to occur more often?

Talking to Teachers Differently When Your Child Has a School Problem

How can you assist your child/adolescent's teachers to approach your child/adolescent in the same successful, respectful manner that Trudy and Terry approached their students? It begins with your approach. As a parent, talking to your child's teacher and informing him/her that you are interested in *assisting the school* **and** *your child* to behave and learn in class is essential. However, the manner in which you approach your child's teacher is crucial. For example, consider the following dialogue told by a mother who was concerned over her child's poor grades and misbehavior:

Mom: "Ms. Smith, I feel you are the expert on my daughter's school life. I know you are upset/concerned/angry/frustrated with Susie's behavior/grade in class. Can you look at your grade book for a moment and see when the times are that she behaves slightly better? Can you notice which subjects she seems to be more successful at? What do you think seems to help her do better? What would you say is the way she learns best, from looking at your book?"

Chances are, Ms. Smith will feel complimented. She is indeed the expert on Susie's academics. However, as in most parent-teacher conferences, Ms. Smith might have come to the conference with a complete list of complaints about Susie, all perfectly warranted. Her complaints would be valid, yet they would offer no solutions. Any suggestions Ms. Smith might give, while focusing on the complaints, would probably be the same suggestions she would give to any other students Susie's age. Sometimes the suggestions work. Other times, parents feel conflictual with the teacher and the defensiveness between the two parties builds a brick wall about ten feet thick between them.

In the same way that Susie plays differently, talks differently and does well in particular subjects, her individuality might conflict with the suggestions Ms. Smith might give. Additionally, it would be Ms. Smith's solutions. For many children/adolescents (and adults), the likelihood of following suggestions from someone they are in conflict with is less likely to happen than if they come up with their own solutions. Remember, one of the major ideas of solution-focused brief therapy is grounded in asking people, "How do you want things to be?" Observe the following questions that could easily apply to school problems. Say to your child/adolescent:

"How would you like things to be for yourself in Ms. Smith's class?"

"When was the last time this occurred, just slightly in her class or in other classes you have had before?"

"What was it that you did, specifically, that helped that to happen?"

"If you could tell Ms. Smith (or another teacher) what she did that made such a difference, what do you wish she knew?"

These questions assist your child/adolescent in becoming responsible for developing his/her own strategies and applying them. In the following cases, observe how a child and two adolescents dealt with their school problems in extraordinary ways, after identifying their unique exceptions.

Case #1: Outlining the Solution

Brent, a troubled high school sophomore, was constantly in trouble at home for his poor school performance. I asked him once how he thought he learned best. He told me he learned best from review sheets. As a matter of fact, in four out of six of his high school subjects, he was able to make grades in the 90s on his tests when his teachers gave review sheets the week before a test. With this information we began to discover together.

LM: "How would you like things to be for yourself?"

Brent: "I'd like my parents to lay off. I'm not as smart as they think I am . . . I can get by but it's hard."

LM: "So, what would it take to get them to lay off?"

Brent: "Pass the classes."

LM: "You told me earlier that you make 90s on some tests because sometimes the teachers give you review sheets. What do the review sheets do for you?"

Brent: "I take them and read them the night before and then again before the test. I always get 90s when I do that."

LM: "Have you had the chance to ask teachers for review sheets or papers before, when they did not give them out?"

Brent: "I didn't know I could do that."

LM: "How might you try to do that?"

Brent: "Well, probably if they thought I was really interested, they would give me notes or something when they didn't pass out review sheets."

LM: "How would they know you were really interested?"

Brent: "Probably I would stay after class and talk to them."

LM: "What else would **they** say would be some small signals that you were really interested in your grade?"

Brent: "Probably turn in all of my homework. See, sometimes I don't do it and then when the tests come up they aren't interested in helping me."

LM: "So, turning in homework and staying after class might begin to show your teachers that you are serious now."

Brent: "Yeah."

I asked Brent:

"How would you like things to be?"

"What would it take to get that to happen?"

"When is it that you are successful?"

"What does that (strategy) do for you that makes a difference?"

"What could you begin to do on a small scale?"

For Brent, review sheets or outlines given to him by his teachers pulled the information together and helped it to make sense to him. His teachers had previously told him to just go home and review the chapter. However, Brent had a slight problem in reading and comprehension, which the outlines clarified for him. He had difficulties organizing the information as well. His idea for improving his grades was to ask the teachers for a review sheet early *every week* or to ask for a copy of the outline they used to lecture to the class.

"Memory is the only paradise from which no one can drive us."

—Jean Paul (Friedrich Richter)

Case #2: "The Answers Are In the Bag"

Tracy, a junior high student, came to talk to me once with his parents who claimed he was the most disorganized adolescent they had ever seen. He would always do his homework (his parents always checked it), yet he would constantly forget to turn in his homework in five out of eight of his classes. As Tracy and I talked, I asked him how he remembered to turn the homework in to three of his classes.

Tracy: "That's easy. When I do my Math, I stick the work in my book and my locker is close to the classroom so I always remember to get the book."

LM: "How does it help for your locker to be so close?"

Tracy: "That's easy. See, my school is big and we don't have enough time to get from class to class without being tardy . . . especially if I see a friend who I want to talk to."

LM: "So, you're saying that when you put your homework in your books, and you have your books, you turn in the homework?"

Tracy: "Yeah. I guess I should take all of my books with me to each class."

Our conversation proceeded similarly to my conversation with Brent. Tracy's parents had tried organizers, tape recorders, different binders to get their son organized—all to no avail. Tracy's solution sounded like a lot of work. But, it worked. His parents bought him an oversized bag and he carried all of his books to class and turned in all of his homework.

"Imagination is more important than knowledge."

—*Albert Einstein*

Beginning to help your child/adolescent's teacher observe your child with a new description, similar to the ways I have described in this book, is the core of the next case. As you read through the case, observe how

Annie changed *her* perception of the teacher and how her mom's involvement assisted her daughter's teacher to watch for something different.

Case #3: "Check Out The Teacher"

Annie, age 9, was referred to me by her school principal for "disruptive talking and belligerent attitude. " She was enrolled in Honors classes in which she excelled with little effort. Bright and articulate, she admitted to me she knew why she was in trouble constantly.

Annie: "My teacher always catches me talking to my friends at our table when we are working. Then, she puts a huge check by my name in front of the entire class. It is so embarrassing. It makes me mad so I just keep on."

LM: "Annie, what is Ms. Johnson missing that you wish she could see?"

Annie: "That I'm nice. I just like to talk to my friends. She's mean to me. I bring home a checklist every day and every day she puts bad things on it. There are always minus signs next to my behavior. That gets me in a lot of trouble at home. Then, she always writes down something mean at the bottom of the page."

Annie's mom: "Her teacher is sometimes negative. I have tried to talk to her and all she does is tell me how we should put Annie in a different class or school. I'm afraid to do that because she does so well in school. Besides, so much has happened over the past few years. I remarried two years ago and recently had a baby. I know I am impatient with Annie, but I need her help sometimes. She and I have begun arguing more and she has become harder to manage at home recently. She probably needs a lot of counseling, too, since she has not seen her real father for almost seven years and she sometimes does not get along with her stepdad.

LM: "Gee, you all have so much happening. Annie, how do you explain how you are able to get such good grades with so much going on?"

Annie: "I just do it."

LM: "Are there times when Ms. Johnson is not being 'mean' to you?"

Annie: "Yeah, when I am doing my work and not talking."

LM: "When else?"

Annie: "Sometimes I help other kids at my table. She never gets on me when she can tell I am working."

LM: "If I read her mind, what would be different during those times?"

Annie: "I guess I don't laugh or anything . . . I just work. I don't talk back. I don't get up from my chair."

LM: "Would you like to do a little experiment? I would like you to give Ms. Johnson something to fill out that is **very different** from the checklist you bring home each day."

At this point, Annie and I completed the form entitled: *"Teacher Observations of 'Good Behavior.'"* After we finished, we brought the paper to show her mom and stepdad. Annie really liked the idea of the form.

LM: "Mom, what I have learned about Annie is that she knows how to have good behavior, but apparently people are missing it. Would you mind, when you return Annie to school this morning, giving this form to Ms. Johnson in front of Annie? Please ask Annie's principal to sign it first, okay?"

Annie's mom: "Sure."

LM: "Annie, you have told me you know how to have good behavior at school; it's just that Ms. Johnson has been **blinded** by the talking that sometimes takes **you** over. So, there's only one thing I want you to do for the next few days. Give Ms. Johnson something new to see to write down on this paper, okay?"

Annie: (Smiling) "Okay."

LM: "Mom, would you mind if Annie brings this home each Friday to show you how she is changing her image in Ms. Johnson's eyes?"

Annie's mom: "Yes! I think, too, as we have talked, I realize that I haven't spent enough time with her lately. In fact, I think I'm too critical sometimes."

LM: "How do you approach people at work whom you need to assist in doing things differently?"

Annie's mom: "Actually, I'm really patient with them."

Annie: "Mom, you used to be patient with me, too."

LM: "When, Annie?"

Annie: "She used to not work so long and she and I would fold clothes together and sometimes I even helped her to put them away . . . we would play a game then."

Annie's mom: (Crying) "She's right. I think I need to begin doing that again."

LM: "Then, since you have come up with such a nice idea, Annie, would you mind watching at home this week for times when Mom is patient with you?"

Annie: "Sure."

LM: "Mom, what would you think about showing Annie the same type of patience you often use at the office?"

Annie's mom: "Good idea."

Annie's Mom gave Ms. Johnson the *"Teacher Observations of 'Good Behavior'"* when they returned to school that morning. An appointment was made for two weeks later. Two weeks later, Annie's stepdad called our office to cancel the appointment. Apparently, Annie's behavior had improved so much that the teacher was complimenting her daily on her improvement. She had improved relationships with other students and she and her mom were getting along better. In a follow-up conversation with Annie two months later, she appeared happy, confident, and completely assured that if she ever encountered a teacher who "failed to see my good points," she would just "show them" who she really was. What occurred in the conversation between myself, Annie, and her mom?

- Annie began to see herself as someone bothered by "talking" instead of as a bad child. This allowed her to take responsibility to get in control of the talking so Ms. Johnson could see the "nice" person she was.

- Annie's mom became more involved with the school process, making herself an assistant of the teacher and Annie by presenting the form to Ms. Johnson, asking for her help, and then encouraging Annie to "show" Ms. Johnson her "nice" side.

- All of the change between Annie and her mom occurred by reminiscing to a time when they got along better. This "resistance buster" allowed Mom to realize that perhaps she needed to spend more time with Annie, who valued her, instead of accusing her of neglecting her.

- Annie became the expert on her changes. Ms. Johnson became the expert on watching for the changes.

Teacher Observations of "Good Behavior"

_____

Principal's Signature

Date: _____

Dear Ms. Johnson,

Annie, her family, and I are interested in the times at school when Annie has **good** behavior. We are trying to assist Annie in being more successful at managing her behavior in school.

During the next week, please watch for times when **good** behavior occurs and write those times down on the lines below. Please be as specific as you can so that Annie will know how to repeat the **good** behavior more often. **Annie will pick up this sheet on Friday.**

Thank you very much!

Annie, Annie's Parents, and Linda Metcalf, Ph.D.

1._____

2._____

3._____

4._____

5._____

_____

Teacher Signature

How to Conduct a Parent Conference Using a Solution-Focused "Attitude"

Stephen Covey, author of *The Seven Habits of Highly Effective People,* states how schools typically teach students and their parents to develop what he refers to as a *Win/Lose* attitude in the following excerpt:

> *"The 'normal distribution curve' basically says that you got an 'A' because someone else got a 'C.' It interprets an individual's value by comparing him or her to everyone else." (Covey, 1990, p. 208)*

This passage exemplifies the typical parent-teacher conference: focusing on what's wrong with the student by comparing him/her with other students and using strategies used by successful students, even if they do not apply. Beginning on page 159 is a *Solution-Focused Individual Education Plan* for parents to complete *before* requesting a parent-teacher conference. This exercise was developed from an *Individual Education Plan (IEP)*. Teachers, school counselors, school psychologists, administrators, and diagnosticians complete IEPs when they are concerned about placing a troubled student in the best possible academic atmosphere. The IEP assists the educator with such placement. Unfortunately, typical IEPs focus on deficits.

This solution-focused IEP, however, focuses on learning styles, effective discipline, teaching methods that work, and interests you can compile prior to the conference. As you fill out the IEP, consult your child/adolescent's recent report card, past report cards, or request to see your child/adolescent's records at the school. Together with using a solution-focused approach while speaking to your child/adolescent's teacher, referring to the IEP, and requesting the teacher observation forms included in this chapter, the conference described later in this chapter will offer you an alternative for your next conference.

How to Schedule the Solution-Focused Parent Conference

Because of the very nature of the solution-focused parent conference, it is necessary to lay some groundwork to maximize your efforts. On the next few pages you will find forms to copy and to give to your child/adolescent's teachers in addition to a list of *guiding ideas for a successful parent-teacher conference.*

The Solution-Focused
Individual Education Plan

Parent: Complete and take this form to the conference.

Name _____   Grade_____   Date _____

A. Present Competencies

1. Physical, as it affects participation in instructional settings:

_____No physical limitations, no modifications of regular class needed

_____Some physical limitations, no modification of regular class needed

_____Needs modifications because of the following impairment:

_____

In what activities does the impairment **not** affect the student?

_____

_____

2. Physical, as it affects physical education:

_____ YES _____ NO   The student is capable of receiving instruction in the essential elements of physical education through the regular program without modifications.

If NO, list the following activities in which the student **has** shown capabilities of receiving instruction:

_____

Recommendation for continuous activities or future activities, based on competency in listed activities:

_____

159

B. Behavioral Competencies

Educational placement and programming:

_____No modifications

_____Has some characteristics that **may** affect learning, although not severe enough to withdraw from regular classes: (check those that may apply) _____ poor task completion _____ impulsive _____ requires reminding to complete work _____distractible _____ may need isolation to concentrate

Situations in which characteristics occur less in the classroom, according to parent, teachers, and student:

_____

Situations in which student is more prone to follow disciplinary rules effectively, according to teachers, student, and parent:

_____

C. Prevocational/Vocational

Skills that may be prerequisite to vocational education. Rate the following skills using a scale of 1 to 10, where 1 = completely unskilled and 10 = completely competent. (Ask your child/adolescent for assistance.)

_____thinking/process skills   _____expressive skills

_____reading level   _____organizational skills

_____performance   _____social skills

_____verbal comprehension   _____follows directions

_____attendance   _____personal hygiene

_____punctual on assignments   _____listening skills

Utilizing all skills with a rating of 6 or above, list opportunities within the school setting that seem appropriate for this student:

_____

_____

D. Academic/Developmental: (Grade or age levels alone are not sufficient).

1. Indicate the content areas in which the student is competent and can receive instruction in the regular or remedial program. (Ask your child/adolescent for assistance.)

___all subjects   ___reading   ___math   ___social studies

___English   ___science   ___spelling   ___computer literacy

___health   ___fine arts   ___phys. ed.   ___vocational

___foreign lang.   ___athletics   ___geography   ___world history

___other: _____

2. Based on the identified subject competencies, list the identified subjects below and a brief explanation of the teaching methods and abilities of the student that contribute to the success in that subject. (Ask your child/adolescent for assistance.)

Subject	Effective Teaching Methods/Abilities of Student

3. List the content areas in which the student's competency development needs assistance and, using the Effective Teaching Methods given in #2, write suggested teaching strategies that might benefit this student. (Ask your child/adolescent for assistance.)

Subject	Suggested Teaching Method

4. List situations at home that influence your child/adolescent to complete homework assignments and be productive in school. Ask your child/adolescent for assistance with these situations. Add other suggestions from #3 that may be useful at home.

_____

_____

_____

Letter of Request For Teacher Information

Date: _____

Dear _____:

    As the expert on _____'s school life, I am trying to assist _____ in being more successful in school. I am attaching a form for your convenience, and would appreciate it if you would watch for any times, even if only occasional, when _____ does slightly better in your class. These observations from you will be important to us because they will give us ideas of what you need to see more often in the classroom. We really appreciate your help.

    I will be attending a conference set up by the administration on _____ at _____ o'clock, to discuss your observations and learn more from your expertise. Please bring the form with you.

Sincerely,

_____
    Parent Signature

Teacher Observations of Academic Success

Name of Student: _____   Date: _____

Subject/Class: _____

Teacher: _____

Please list at least 2 activities in which the student was able to achieve at least partial success. Please mention what the student did to be successful and the teaching method used. Please rate the student's progress on a scale of 1 to 10, with 1 = not successful and 10 = completely competent.

Activity #1: _____

Performance:_____

Teaching Method: _____

Rating:_____

Activity #2: _____

Performance:_____

Teaching Method: _____

Rating:_____

Activity #3: _____

Performance:_____

Teaching Method: _____

Rating:_____

Teacher Observations of Good Behavior

Name of Student: _____   Date: _____

Subject/Class: _____

Teacher: _____

Please list below at least two situations in which the student was able to follow your disciplinary plan and show you good behavior. Please mention specifically what the student did to earn your respect and what was occurring in your classroom that may have assisted the student to have good behavior.

1. _____

   _____

   _____

2. _____

   _____

   _____

3. _____

   _____

   _____

Guiding Ideas for Planning a Successful Parent-Teacher Conference

1. Complete the IEP. Copy the "Teacher Observations of Good Behavior" or "Teacher Observations of Academic Success" forms, whichever page applies to your son/daughter's situation. Make enough copies for each of your child/adolescent's teachers. Do not be afraid to use these forms for your older adolescent. I have given these forms to teachers of high school seniors who benefited greatly from their teachers' comments.

2. Contact your school vice principal, headmaster, or school counselor and request that he/she sign the letter at the top. Take the forms personally to the teachers' secretary or take them personally to the teachers. Allow a week for the teachers to observe your child/adolescent. Attach a letter similar to the "Letter of Request" or copy the letter form and fill in the blanks for your convenience.

3. The day of the conference, take the IEP to the conference and request that your child/adolescent attend the conference as it concludes. Speak to your school administrator or school counselor about which administrator will sit in on the conference. Absolutely request this! Mention to the administrator how you want to work with the teachers **differently.**

   As the conference begins, get everyone's version of the problem first. Then, ask them to examine their observation forms. Use your IEP as a reference for the way in which your child learns/listens/behaves best. Ask the teachers to consider your discoveries.

4. It is advisable that your son/daughter not attend until you have the chance to hear the teachers' version of the problem and their observations of "exceptions" from the observation forms. When you have compiled a list of times when your child/adolescent's teachers say your child is at least partially successful, invite your child/adolescent in to the meeting. This helps to lessen resistance with the student (and lessens him/her hearing negative remarks) and helps pronounce your intentions of only focusing on productive strategies from the exceptions. This may take time and effort on your part to help the teachers to work with you.

Should the teachers continue to talk about the deficits, thank them for their ideas and say:

- *"What would you like to see _____ doing **instead?**"*
- *"When does that happen ever so slightly?"*

Or, if a teacher simply cannot think of any exceptions, ask:

- *"When is this problem the very worst?"*
- *"From that description, when is it slightly better?"*

If you **still** do not get a productive answer, say:

- *"I know this is a different way of talking about my son/daughter."*
- *"Would you mind, for the next week, watching again, for any time when he/she does slightly better?"*

Remember, you are asking teachers to change their thinking. Be patient. Keeping this in mind, when your son/daughter enters the room, turn to your child/adolescent and say:

> *"Ms. Smith is having a difficult time seeing the times when things go better in class. It looks like you will really need to show her something different during the next week. What do you think she might need to see?"*

5. Then turn to all of the teachers and mention the "exceptions" you have been discussing with your son/daughter in front of the teachers. Before the conference ends, ask your son/daughter what he/she thinks would be helpful for the teachers to do in the classroom. Ask what he/she thinks the teachers might need to see him/her do more of during the next week. Let the teachers know you will check back with those who are concerned the most about your son/daughter at the end of the next week.

6. Before ending, give each teacher 3 × 5 cards with a scale of 1 to 10, similar to the one shown on page 167. This is a particularly enjoyable exercise for students in grades K-8.

What's Working In School This Week . . .

name of student: _____   week:_____

unsuccessful _____successful
        1   2   3   4   5   6   7   8   9   10

Teachers are busy people, yet circling numbers can be quick and productive. Ask the teachers to visit with your child each week and ask him/her:

"Where do you think you are on the scale this week?"

"I (teacher) think you are at _____ because..."

If your child/adolescent did not move up, but instead, moved down, ask the teachers to ask:

"What did you do last week that seemed to get you a higher score?"

"What do you think might move you up next week?"

This is a simple method that eliminates paperwork for both teacher and student, and encourages more of a partnership between student and teacher. Before you end the conference, ask the teachers to mark on the card where they think your child/adolescent is on the scale. Ask your child/adolescent where he/she is on the scale. Mention that you are hoping for a small step towards a "10" just for a week. Before the conference ends, glance at your child/adolescent and say:

"Give them something different to see just for a week, and watch what your teachers are doing that seems to help you."

Mention to the teachers that your child/adolescent will pick up the cards each Friday (or whenever you choose).

When your child/adolescent brings home the cards, write thank-you notes to teachers whom you see really making an effort. Encourage your child/adolescent to write them with you or, if this sounds too silly to him/her, write the notes anyway and mail them to the school. Thank them for their efforts in doing something different.

Summary of the Conference

1. *Ask for an administrator to be present.*

2. *Ask for everyone's version of the problem.*

3. *Ask for everyone's exceptions, saying you are interested in assisting them and your child/adolescent at school and the exceptions give you clues as to how to accomplish that.*

4. *Compile a list of the exceptions from everyone.*

5. *Bring in your child/adolescent and read the list of exceptions to him/her. Ask him/her to tell everyone what he/she needs in school.*

6. *Tell your child/adolescent to show the teachers something different for just a week and that the teachers will be watching. Ask your child to also watch what the teachers will be doing that seems to help him/her.*

7. *Pass out 3 × 5 cards to teachers in grades K-8. For older adolescents, ask the teachers to mention successes personally to the adolescents or write them a note.*

8. *Write thank-you notes to teachers who do things differently and encourage your child/adolescent's success.*

Concluding Comments

The activities in this chapter are designed to give you the opportunity to see your child/adolescent's teachers differently. These exercises also promote good school-home relationships and encourage your son/daughter to take responsibility for changing his/her school life. The activities do not ask anyone to invent new strategies for your child/adolescent to do, lessening stress on teachers and eliminating blaming between home and school. Instead, the exercises allow your child/adolescent to become the successful person he/she is meant to be, learning more about himself/herself in the process. When a person learns early in life how he/she learns best, the gift lasts a lifetime *and can be used in many situations!* As a familiar Native American saying reminds us:

> *"Give a man a fish, and you feed him for a day;*
> *teach him to fish—and you feed him for a lifetime."*
>
> —*Native American saying*

Chapter
7

Talking to Kids During Times of Crisis

*"There is no exercise better for the heart
than reaching down and lifting people up."*

—*John Andrew Holler*

What do you do when the daughter you adore loses her self-respect and tearfully longs for its return? What do you do when you watch your child mourn for the loss of someone he loved so dearly . . . your heart breaking along with his? How do you deal with the ever-increasing pressures of gang involvement on a son who desires so dearly to *belong* . . . how do you intervene to save his life and . . . your relationship with him? How do you preserve the mental health of an adolescent who loves drugs as much as she loves her family?

In times of crisis, we all look for answers to solve these painful experiences quickly and most of the time that means looking at what *caused* the crisis. In this chapter, a different approach evolves. Instead of looking for the *root of the problem,* the parents, children, and adolescents described looked within themselves for answers instead of searching for *why* the crisis occurred in the first place. You will meet within these pages strong families who were determined to win back their children and adolescents from some of the worst circumstances plaguing young people today. Enjoy their new legacies and watch for the creative ways in which they *loved their children back to health.*

Crisis #1: Reclaiming Self-Respect from a "Situation"

Anna's parents thought they had done everything right. They had taken their three children to church every Sunday, gone on countless family picnics and vacations, given them encouragement and praise, and always participated in their school activities. They gave them their best and they expected nothing in return but their children's happiness. Anna was the apple of her dad's eye, enjoying conversations on everything from relationships to scuba diving; they respected each other and spent ample time together.

Everything changed the day Anna's mom picked her up from school early, only to find Anna and her boyfriend behind the school building in a sexual situation. Astounded and angry, the respect and trust for Anna that her parents had developed over fifteen years dissolved—or so it seemed—in only one afternoon. Her father drove with Anna to her boyfriend's home immediately upon learning of the incident, and told the young man's parents about the crisis. To the young man, Anna's father appeared furious and decisive, and her father told him that he was never to see his daughter in a social situation again. While Anna cried many tears that day, she seemed to realize she had much repair work to do to earn her parents' trust again.

Meeting the family for the first time, I was impressed that everyone (Anna, her father, and her mother) was present to talk about the "crisis" that had occurred. The family had come to talk to me, thinking that Anna needed therapy to get back on the right track. Anna, subdued and quiet, showed great remorse for what she had done as we talked individually, yet she did not completely understand why her parents had taken the drastic actions they did. As I talked to her about the normal feelings she had for her boyfriend, she finally told me he had pushed her into the situation, and it wasn't the first time it had happened. She explained that he had pushed for more but she always had the ability to say "no." At this point, she felt shameful and had lost her self-respect. When I asked her how she wanted things to be so her life would be back to some kind of "normalcy," the following conversation took place:

Anna: "I want my parents to trust me again. I'm really a nice person. I don't normally do things like this. . . . I just felt pressured to do more than I wanted so that he would stay my boyfriend. I don't like sneaking around."

LM: "How would you like things to be, considering this crisis has occurred?"

Anna: "I want my parents to see me as a good person. I want their trust back. They probably don't trust me at all anymore."

LM: "I wonder what your parents might say would raise your trust level with them."

Anna: "I guess they would have to know that I wasn't going to do anything like that again."

LM: "How would they know?"

Anna: "Well, it seems pretty easy. . . . They won't let me see him anymore, so that's not the issue. I guess they might see it if I dated people who didn't push me into doing things I didn't really want to do."

LM: "In your opinion, what would you be doing around different guys that would show your parents they were different from your ex-boyfriend?"

Anna: "They wouldn't ask me to sneak around and I would say 'no' when it did not feel right. I wouldn't get in a situation where that could happen either. I would avoid those situations. Actually, it made me feel cheap. He didn't want to be close to me unless I would so something (sexually) with him. I didn't like that. . . . I just did it because he said he wouldn't hang around me if I didn't."

LM: "So, what would the other guys do instead of that?"

Anna: "They would like me for me. They would also like being around my parents. They would listen to me when I said I didn't like something they did to me. I would be more in control, I guess."

At this point, I invited Anna's parents to come back into the room with Anna and me. Together, we drew on a piece of paper what I referred to as "a trust thermometer." I asked Anna's mom and dad about the times before this incident when they trusted Anna.

LM: "On this thermometer, a '10' means you totally trusted your daughter and a '1' means there was no trust. Where would you both say she was before this incident?"

Dad: "Probably a 9."

Mom: "At least an 8."

LM: "Anna, where do you think you are now?"

Anna: "I'm probably in the minuses."

LM: "Dad and Mom, where would you put her now?"

Dad: "About a 3."

Mom: "Yes, about a 2."

LM: "So, in spite of this situation, you still trust her slightly? How do you do that?"

Dad: "Because I know who she really is. She is a respectable girl who got mixed up with a jerk. She and I have always been close and it doesn't seem to fit. We've talked about sex and when it's right countless times. I told her I remember how it was being a teenage boy myself. But after all of this, I can't just stop trusting her completely, even though I'm very concerned."

Mom: "It's true, Anna is a good kid who I found in a bad situation. I don't like it that she let herself get into that situation, and I blame her for being in it. But, I still love her and know she deserves to be treated better."

LM: "The way that you intervened, Dad, and went to her boyfriend's house . . . is that typical of how you commonly react to times when your kids are in trouble?"

Dad: "Absolutely. I always take some kind of action to protect them, and they know it's not to trap them or anything, just take care of them. Then we talk about it and they know where their mother and I stand. While we have never had to deal with anything like this, we always do something. . . . We never just let it go and say, 'Oh, well, they will have to work it out for themselves, or, they can just leave.' We always do something."

LM: "This is really nice to hear and apparently it has worked for you. Anna is 15 and until now, it sounds like for 14.9 years, she has proven to you that you could indeed trust her. I am glad to hear that you both used the skills you have developed so far to help get Anna back on track."

With Anna's permission I told her family that she desired, more than anything else, to win back their respect for her. For Anna this would mean she also regained some freedom, yet her parents' respect and the idea of lessening their hurt were primary to her. It occurred to me at that moment that the years of communication, family togetherness, and efforts **had** paid off to her parents at this point. Instead of being rebellious and belligerent, Anna was able to see beyond her needs for a boyfriend, and look to the people who had given her life as knowledgeable and protective instead of confrontational and restricting.

LM: "Mom and Dad, on that same thermometer, what would it take for Anna to move up slightly during the next week?"

Dad: "Stay away from the boyfriend at school. I plan on being at home after school with her or her mother will be there so she is not put in any tough situation again. In addition (glancing at Anna) I might just appear and disappear at school once or twice during the next few weeks." (Apparently Anna had told her parents that her boyfriend had followed her home from school before and coerced her into opening the door for him.)

Mom: "I agree, plus I would like to see her participating more in church activities again. Since she met this boy, she has dropped out of some activities and her grades have dropped as well. I want that to improve."

LM: "So, that would be a beginning. Anna, what do you think you might do to move up, in addition to what your parents just described?"

Anna: "All of that sounds fine. I didn't realize they still trusted me a little, and that makes me feel a lot better. I am really surprised at that. I just need to do more to convince them that I think more of myself than what they saw that day."

The Anatomy of a Crisis

Crisis situations that scar one's self respect in order to keep a boyfriend, make better grades, or become popular confirm that there are pressures in childhood/adolescence that can often throw kids off track. Kids—even good kids—get into trouble. In Anna's case, her parents really did not need therapy; they needed reassurance. They were able and wise enough to see their daughter's worth and to take charge of the situation, proving to her that she was worth more. By taking "action," as described by her father, her parents did not criticize Anna; they simply took her to a higher ground, sending a message that "you are better than this." It seemed to work.

What did Anna's parents do to assist her through the crisis?

1. **They provided an atmosphere where she always knew she was loved.** Prior to the "situation," the family atmosphere was always open and accepting, communication was good, acceptance and validation were always given, and the kids knew their parents had their best interest at heart. They knew they were important because their parents always made time for them. This "preventive" setting made dealing with the crisis slightly easier as Anna was already used to processing and discussing issues, even uncomfortable ones, with her family.

2. **They respectfully told her that her actions were not acceptable.** The parents told their daughter that the actions she participated in were not acceptable and took an additional step of action to assist in preventing it from happening again. This was their typical intervention over the years and they relied on past experiences and interventions that had worked before to help them through the current situation.

3. **They separated her from the problem.** They recognized her "exceptions" foremost. They never lost total trust for their daughter.

Instead, they were able to look at her as a person and separate her from the actions. This encouraged Anna to be less defensive, even though she still had consequences.

4. **They took the responsibility and the risk to show her the values in their family.** They saw their daughter as their responsibility and were willing to supervise her so she could "regain" her values. This sent a message to Anna that "I am special."

Sometimes Kids Get Stuck . . . And Sometimes They Don't!

In this chapter, I will attempt to share many situations in which parents and kids find themselves in a crisis. As each story unfolds, watch for the abilities each parent or child/adolescent had that assisted them toward finding solutions. Notice how finding the exceptions led them to solutions. Sometimes the "exceptions" were well hidden in past accomplishments, yet when recognized, led to strategies that were both comfortable and successful in stepping out of the crisis.

It is very common when I work with parents to first hear complaints about the problem or crisis at hand, then later, how "basically good" their kids have always been. The latter is important vital information to remember in times of crisis. It is very easy to only see the current upsetting situation. What is important to point out to your child/daughter is that you do remember times when he/she was responsible and trouble-free. By verbalizing these facts, your child/adolescent is more likely to "think" about what he/she did and receive the consequences in a less rebellious way. This is the ideal situation. Consequences should *teach,* not criticize and demean kids.

The questions below may be helpful to parents to think about if/when a crisis occurs. Review them privately or with your partner *before* talking to your child/adolescent:

Step #1: Questions to Think About Before Taking "Action" in Times of Crisis (Ideas to help you calm down first!)

1. *How do I want the conversation I am about to have with my son/daughter to turn out? What is my purpose in having the conversation? (To criticize or assist him/her in learning and growing more responsible?)*

2. *What strategies have I used before that seemed to work in getting across my point so that he/she listened to my **concerns?** (Ask your partner or review past situations through your kids' eyes.)*

3. *What do I basically know about my child/adolescent's values or beliefs? Knowing them, how might this influence how I might talk to him/her?*

4. *How often do crises occur with my child/adolescent compared with how often successes occur?*

5. *If I looked through my child/adolescent's eyes, what would I discover about what this negative situation **did** (or was supposed to do) for him/her? Did he/she feel accepted, part of the crowd, have fun, feel obligated, feel daring, want to acquire praise, etc?*

6. *If you were your child/adolescent, what would you hope your parent understood? Remember, understanding the situation does not mean you shouldn't give consequences, it just "helps the medicine go down" easier when you have a chance to explain that you are trying to understand the situation.*

Step #2: Make the Conversation an Intervention

As you talk with your child/adolescent during a crisis situation, attempt to make the conversation an intervention in itself. There is no research that says lectures, threats, or "grounded for the rest of your life" ever really work. Who would want to try after that? Most kids whom I see in counseling tell me that it is their parents' opinion of them when they are in trouble that hurts the most. Even the kids who have terrible relationships with their family tell me the same. They desperately want acceptance, yet are too inexperienced to know how to get it . . . so they go the opposite direction. We need to be facing them from the opposite direction, receiving them openly.

To accomplish this enormous and very important task, recall your strengths, abilities, and competencies in other tough situations. How do you remain calm, for example, in a confrontation at work? How do you and your spouse work our differences at times? Consider how you keep your cool (at times) in other situations and prepare for another similar situation with your child/adolescent. Then, with all of your resources, attempt to teach that very important young person a way to get back on track. Below are some questions you might consider using to process the situation at hand. Notice how the questions focus on identifying when the problem could not occur.

Ask: "Tell me your view of the problem and how it occurred."

When you discover that your child/adolescent has gotten "off track," keep a cool, yet concerned attitude for him/her while asking for his/her view of the problem. Listen attentively and ask for many details so you understand fully what occurred, even if you think your child/adolescent is not being totally truthful.

Ask: "What do you think I need to see that will tell us both that this situation will not occur anymore?"

This question allows your child/adolescent to take responsibility for the actions that led to the crisis. By phrasing it in terms of what you need to see, you take the blame off your child/adolescent and allow him/her to think of a solution-focused goal, even if you hear a reply of: "It wasn't my fault so I don't know."

Ask: "Okay, suppose I took a video camera and taped you when this problem was going on. If I taped you on another day when the problem was not happening, what would be different from the first tape?"

The purpose of this question is to help your son/daughter clarify what events took place and their participation in them. After you help your child/adolescent identify how they would not participate in the problem, it is easy to design strategies to avoid it in the future.

Ask: "What small steps would I see you taking over the next week that would convince you and I that you could avoid this happening again? What else? What else? What else?"

Then ask: "What could I do to assist you that could help you to accomplish that?"

Notice that I added three "what else?" questions. Usually when problems occur, there are many reasons for it occurring. By asking "what else?" you give your child/adolescent a chance to think of all the strategies they might take to avoid the problem next time. This brainstorming is very helpful since it will assist your child/adolescent to consider people, places, and situations that need avoidance.

Notice also, a short period of time is given in which to prove that he/she is capable of avoiding the problem. This makes success achievable.

*Do not be concerned that you are asking your child/adolescent to show **you** what you need to see. Children and young adolescents have a difficult time thinking of good moral reasons why something should not happen again. You are their resource. Your validation and acceptance is important. While they may at first attempt to please you, give **them** total credit for getting back on track.*

State: "I appreciate your willingness to come up with some ideas. What I need you to know is that I will be watching for your ability to keep the problem from happening during the next week. I will also help you avoid it by . . ." (action)

This statement requires two things:

a. *new thoughts (and actions) that help you create an environment in which your child/adolescent is less likely to participate in the problem*

b. *old skills that have proven effective in dealing with your child/adolescent in the past*

Yes, it takes preparation. These conversations are perhaps the most important presentations or projects you will ever do. Your audience may be defensive and skeptical. Your actions and words should match your intention—to assist your child/adolescent in growing up healthy and responsible. A businessman would never deliver a strategy that he did not design beforehand, so you should plan your intervention. If your child/adolescent cannot come up with strategies during the first conversation, take a raincheck and ask him/her to:

"Think about what has occurred and what you and I would see you doing the next time a similar situation occurs and you do not participate. Tell me about it tomorrow evening."

After you process, notice the days when your child/adolescent is problem-free, and tell him/her you noticed. Refrain from saying, "I'm just waiting for it to happen again." This accomplishes nothing. Refrain from bringing up old crisis situations as a reminder that he/she has been in trouble before. If your boss read a litany of work-related failures to you, how motivated would you be to do better tomorrow? Instead, focus on problem-free days . . . leave notes on your kids' bathroom vanity, their pillow, in their lunch bag. Helping kids see themselves differently will help them act differently.

Crisis #2: Helping Your Kids When Their Loved Ones Pass Away (as suggested by the work of Michael White, 1989)

Joan, age 16, had adored her friend, Robert, who passed away at the young age of 28 last year. Together they enjoyed picnics with her family and their friendship eventually took on a role of brother and sister, giving Joan a sounding board after her older brother went off to college. Robert helped Joan with her Algebra and Spanish homework and she, in turn, took time to read to him after his eyesight failed him during his illness. They were close and his influence on Joan enriched her self-esteem and encouraged her to do well in school. After he died during the fall of that year, Joan became lethargic and depressed, her grades fell, and she lacked any insight as to how to move on in her life.

As I talked with Joan, she told me her family had also undergone a critical situation during the last year. Her dad had lost his job and her mom had gone back to work and had begun night school to finish her college degree. Additionally, her big brother had gone off to college and chose to spend his summer working in his college town. Joan had two part-time jobs to help with the family income, yet still maintained A's and B's in school, was on the track team, and helped out at home on the weekends. She was obviously a young woman who could deal with transitions.

Joan said she knew she had to "forget and go on," but she just couldn't. I then said to her:

LM: "Then, let's not move on right away. Tell me, as you look back at Robert, what were the influences he had on your life?"

Joan: (Smiling) "He showed me how to have fun, even though he was in a wheelchair most of the time. We would go out to the lake and just talk about . . . everything!"

LM: "What did that do for you?"

Joan: "Well, I felt like someone understood me. . . . I was feeling pretty mixed up then. I used to collect flowers while we talked and he would make me think about my future and what I wanted. There really wasn't anyone else who would do that like he did."

LM: "It sounds like he was a profound influence on you. Just for a moment, let's imagine you are looking through Robert's eyes right now. When you do this, what abilities would you be noticing that you could appreciate?"

Joan: (Smiling) "Well, I guess he would say that I was smart and could do well in school, and that I am funny sometimes."

LM: "What difference do you think it would make in how you go through your days right now, if you appreciated this about yourself?"

Joan: "I'd probably get up and stop feeling so bad, and get back to work at school. It's just that I miss him so much."

LM: "I know, so let's think about including his 'influence' in your day, each day, as if he was still having this good influence on you at school, at home, at work, like he did just a year ago."

Joan: "You mean I don't have to put him outside of my mind?"

LM: "It sounds like he was too important to you to do that."

Joan: "He was."

LM: "What difference do you think it might make on the rest of this week if you were to go through each day thinking about how Robert saw you and you did the things he influenced you to do?"

Joan: "I've got this history project (laughing) that has to get finished and I haven't even started yet. I would do that."

LM: "What else?"

Joan: "I think I would go back out to the lake to study, where we used to study together. . . . I like it there."

LM: "What do you think your mom or dad would see different in you during this week that would tell them you were discovering the nice things that Robert saw in you?"

Joan: "They would see me smiling again. . . . I don't seem to do that much anymore."

Gaining Peacefulness After Loss

Throughout this book, I have mentioned countless times the importance of cooperating with kids to regain their cooperation. In no other situation is this as important as when kids lose someone they are close to through death. Children/adolescents are often told they must put that person behind them and live through the pain in order to heal. They are told to forget. Michael White wrote a wonderful article entitled "Saying Hullo Again: The Incorporation of the Lost Relationship in the Resolution of Grief." In that article, he quotes Myerhoff (1986):

> *"Freud . . . suggests that the completion of the mourning process requires that those left behind develop a new reality which no longer includes what has been lost. But . . . it must be added that full recovery from mourning may restore what has been lost, maintaining it through incorporation into the present. Full recollection and retention may be as vital to recovery and well-being as forfeiting memories. (1982, p. 110).*

It makes sense to think of the gains from relationships and how those gains can continue to influence persons after that relationship ends in death. The following set of questions are suggested if your child/adolescent has an unfortunate loss to deal with.

Regaining Happiness Through Remembering
Questions and Statements to Assist Kids With Grief and Loss
(#1–6 adapted from Michael White)

1. *I know how much you miss _____. I miss him/her too. I remember so many wonderful things about him/her. If you looked through _____'s eyes for a minute, what would you see in yourself that you could appreciate?*

2. *What do you think might happen if you began to appreciate this in yourself right now?*

3. *What do you think about or remember when you "bring alive" the enjoyable things that _____ knew about you? What do you remember doing when he/she enjoyed watching you do those things?*

4. *What if you were to live in this "influence" (or good memory) of _____ for a day or so and you imagined him/her enjoying watching you again. What might I see you doing?*

5. *What difference would it make when you began doing these things again?*

6. *What do you think others would see when you "reclaimed" some of the discoveries that _____ enjoyed watching you do?*

7. *On a scale of 1 to 10, with 10 = you feel the happiest and 1 = you feel very sad, where were you today before we talked? Where are you now? (For a very young child, suggest that he/she hold out his/her arms fully for a 10 and close together for a 1.) What did we talk about that seemed to help?*

Each day, ask the child/adolescent where he/she is on the scale. If he/she falls backwards slightly, ask how he/she was able to move upward two days ago, for example. Add your own observations and, whenever you notice him/her participating in activities that their loved one would have appreciated, verbalize your discovery with statements such as:

> *"You seem to really be remembering how much _____ loved it when you did that. What fun! How are you doing this?"*

These questions and statements emphasize cooperating with the feelings of loss. Through *redescription* of the loss as an *influence or positive memory,* kids can merge what they loved about their loved one with their own lives, creating happier circumstances. The process takes time, yet these questions seem to cooperate with the pain, thereby lessening the struggle of putting the past behind. The process encourages the past to come forward and follow the child/adolescent into the future.

Crisis #3: Stepping Out of the Trauma of Abuse

William O'Hanlon suggests that therapy for sexual abuse should focus on "possibilities" instead of "working through the gory details." Below are some ideas from O'Hanlon (1994) that suggest strategies for parents to take should their child/adolescent experience such an unfortunate event:

1. Make sure the abuse has stopped. If it has not, call an abuse hotline to report the abuse.

2. Don't assume your child/adolescent has to go back and work through the traumatic event. Many children/adolescents prefer to put the event behind them and are too embarrassed to discuss the details. Compliment them for coming forward and assure them that they are safe.

3. Recall the natural abilities of your child/adolescent as he/she has coped with the abuse. Realize that he/she has continued to go to school, dress nicely, and participate in activities, and verbalize these discoveries.

4. Look for resources and strengths. Focus on underlining how they made it through the abuse and what they have done to cope, survive, and thrive since then. Look for nurturing and healthy relationships and role models they had in the past or have now. Look for skills in other areas.

5. Validate and support each part of the person's experience.

6. Do not give the message that the person is "damaged goods" or that his/her future is determined by having been abused in the past. Remember that change can occur in the interpretations associated with the event.

7. Gently challenge self-blaming or invalidating stories the person has accepted about himself/herself.

Creating a New Focus: Victim No More . . . Hello, Survivor!

Oftentimes, when parents bring their children or adolescents to talk to me about the trauma, they have been told that their children must retell their story. Their parents are also determined to make sure the abuse incidents will never resurface again in their memory so that they will lead normal lives. This is a very tall order to fill. After working with sexual abuse survivors and physical abuse survivors (even verbal abuse fits here), I have learned that retelling the story often contributes to more feelings of powerlessness, blaming oneself for the abuse and resentment towards persons who did not *know* to rescue them from the abuse. Instead, as O'Hanlon states above, it seems more important to assist the person with changing their perception of himself/herself. While professional help can assist you, in addition, parents might consider the following exercise, which intends to help kids see themselves as "escaping from the abuse," down the road towards freedom:

Clearing the Path for Freedom from "The Event"

1. *Mention that you are impressed that in spite of the "event," your child/adolescent continued to live his/her life, participate in activities, and not allow the abuse to take him/her away from all of that. Ask:*

   "How were you able to do that?"

2. Draw a line, such as the one below. Notice on one end is "birth" and the opposite end is "80 years." Place an "x" on the line approximately where the abuse occurred:

   birth____x_____80 years

   Then say:

   "I'm going to draw a line. On one end I'm going to put your birthday. Tell me, about how long do people live in your family? (80 years, perhaps) Now, how old were you when this 'event' stopped? I'm going to put a mark at that point. What shall we call the 'event' that bothered you?"

   Suggestions: a trap, a black cloud, a jail. (Place the name above the "x." From this point on, refer to that name.)

   "What I want you to do for a moment is to imagine with me that in your mind, you are 'stepping out of the _____.' (name) As you do this, I want you to see that from this point on, you have (60-70) years left to never return to the ___. As a matter of fact, you have already moved this far (point from the day the abuse stopped to the current time, approximately)."

   "As you imagine stepping out of the _____, how will this free you? What will you get to do in each day of your life that you move farther and farther away, <u>never</u> going backwards? What will others see you doing?"

3. *Set goals with the child/adolescent by asking:*

   "During the next week, if I were to watch you, what would I see you doing that would tell both of us that you had stepped away from the _____ just a little bit?"

These questions assist the child/adolescent to visually emerge from the "event" and move onward, toward life without the influence of the event. After talking with your son/daughter using these questions, watch for any times when he/she "escapes" from the event and seems to be getting back into life. Consider writing a card or letter to your child/adolescent, modifying it for the person's age, such as the one below:

Dear Susan,

As I watched you play with Stephanie yesterday, I noticed how happy you seemed. Obviously, you are much stronger than the "event" (name) ever was. It was nowhere to be found! I'm happy and very impressed with you. I look forward to your telling me how you have grown so much stronger!

Love,

Mom

The key points in the letter emphasize:

a. the parent's amazement of the child's **escape** from the event

b. the specific events observed by the parent

c. the parent's **curiosity** regarding how the child/adolescent escaped. This is very different from saying "you did a good job escaping today." By being curious about your child/adolescent, you give him/her the credit for the success. This will perhaps encourage more "escaping."

Crisis #4: The "Mom Police" Take on the Gang . . . Ideas to Discourage Your Kids from Gang Involvement

She was told by her family members that her fourteen-year-old son was a member of a gang at school. Shocked, frightened, and concerned, the mother of Paul contacted the mother of his best friend, Sean, and went to her home that same afternoon. Talking about the obvious changes that both of their sons had recently shown towards them, their changes in clothing to "colors," both moms decided they could not waste a minute to rescue their sons. Together, they decided upon a strategy. They would pick up the boys at school and bring them back to talk to them that same afternoon. Nervous that her son would deny the accusations, Jean, a single parent, took matters into her own hands and confronted her own son saying:

> *"Paul, I got an anonymous phone call today. The caller said that you are involved in a gang. I trust this person who called and I know you are involved. I'm not going to let you be involved. You and Sean are leaders already and you don't need to be led. Being involved with a gang would involve your being with people who would hurt all of us."*

After Paul's mom spoke, Sean's mom spoke. The two parents decided to create what they told their sons was the "mom police." The moms would take turns picking up their sons after school and promptly taking them home. They also threw away any items of clothing that resembled "colors" of other gang memberships. After two weeks, the boys were given some of their privileges back and were allowed to walk home several times per week, yet were constantly monitored on their whereabouts in all other situations.

What made the difference with Paul and Sean, so that they cooperated with their mothers' expectations of dropping out of gang involvement?

1. Prior to the situation, Paul and his mother enjoyed a relationship in which he listened to her. He respected her thinking and her attempts to provide a normal, happy life for him and his younger brother. Paul's mother was always *there* for him, and observant of him. After she learned of his involvement, she wasted *no* time to correct the situation. In her words, once she reached a certain point, Paul knew it and he knew he should listen.

2. The mothers praised their sons' abilities. By telling them they were already leaders who did not need to be led, they lessened resistance, restored their confidence (gangs, by the way, work on the same principle of giving confidence to their members), and told them of the dangers that could occur if they continued to be involved. This *reality check* does not always occur with adolescents, who are self-centered, naturally, and have difficulty seeing the consequences on others of what they might do.

3. The mothers took action—they changed the system in which the boys lived. Instead of walking home, they were picked up. Instead of allowing them to wear clothes that spoke their identity, they threw those away that hinted toward gang colors.

4. They allowed the boys to regain **some** privileges after proving they were free of gang involvement. They were allowed to accomplish this in a short amount of time. This strategy allowed the boys to see that there was a way to emerge from the trouble and they were told how to do so.

5. Paul's mom also knew what worked with Paul: calmness, patience, and firm statements that she loved him but did not like what he was doing. Paul also knew that Mom always followed through with consequences.

After the crisis was over, Paul and Sean emerged free of gang involvement and onward to new involvements in sports, where they still remain today. When their parents saw their new involvements, they praised Paul and Sean and allowed the new situations to reassure them that their sons were on the right paths. Paul's and Sean's parents continue to keep watch for other situations in which they both become uncomfortable and do not hesitate to talk or become the "mom police" whenever necessary.

Crisis #5: Drugs No More! A Family Gathers Together to Fight Back

Theresa was a fifteen-year-old who liked to live on the edge. Dressed in what her mom referred to as "freak" type makeup and baggy clothes, she was an adolescent who loved marijuana almost as much as she loved her family. It came as quite a surprise to Theresa's parents when she repeatedly tested positive for marijuana. Her grades had declined, she began skipping school repeatedly, her friends had changed (to all drug abusers), and she became more hostile to her parents.

In our first meeting, Theresa vowed she would never give up pot. She loved the way it made her feel when she listened to music, watched movies, was with friends, you name it . . . she had experienced it with pot. Her parents had asked me to assist them in helping Theresa get straight. From my assessment of the situation, it seemed that Theresa had a daily habit smoking pot and it seemed to be physiologically affecting her sleeping habits, eating habits, mental acuity, grades, and social skills. Everyone noticed this but Theresa. Talking with her, the following dialogue developed.

LM: "Your parents seem very concerned about you. What do you think it will take for them to stop worrying?"

Theresa: "Stop smoking pot . . . but I'm not going to do that."

LM: "How would you like things to be?"

Theresa: "I want my freedom back. Since they found out that I smoke pot, they have taken everything from me. I can't go anywhere, see any friends, spend the night with any girlfriends, it's bad."

LM: "So, does this mean that you have smoked pot less lately since they have taken freedom away?"

Theresa: "Yes, it's pretty hard to do it when you can't go anywhere."

LM: "How long has it been since you smoked pot?"

Theresa: "One week."

LM: "How did you get through the week?"

Theresa: "It was not easy, but I listened to music and ate."

LM: "I understand that you want your freedom back. What do you think it would take for your parents to give you back some more freedom?"

Theresa: "They told me a negative drug screen."

LM: "I wonder how you would get that to happen?"

After this brief conversation, I learned from Theresa that I would not be very effective trying to convince her to stop using marijuana. Her family was going to prove to be more convincing. I knew this because after this conversation, I had the next conversation with her parents:

LM: "Have there been other situations in the past where you saw that your daughter was doing something harmful and you helped her to stop?"

Mom: "Yes, smoking."

LM: "How did you stop her from smoking?"

Mom: "She likes to buy clothes, so we told her that we would pay her $500 to stop smoking. She stopped."

LM: "So, bribing her worked. Have there been other times when you were able to get Theresa on track after she got off track?"

Dad: "I tend to take more of a supervisory role. Before, when she was going out with friends we didn't approve of, we invited them into our home and kept a very close eye on them. She eventually began bringing other, better friends home as well."

LM: "So, giving her a reward and supervising her worked?"

Mom and Dad: "Yes."

LM: "How will you know when things are better for you, Theresa, and your family?"

Mom: "When she has a negative drug screen."

Theresa: "That's going to be hard because I'm not going to totally quit."

LM: "Theresa is saying that she wants her freedom back and you are saying that you expect a negative drug screen. If we were to just begin accomplishing some of these goals, what would you all settle for?"

Dad: "A decreased percentage of pot in her next drug screen."

Mom: "That's hard. I guess a decrease but more time with us. She has become so withdrawn and tired that we never see her. She and I used to do things together and now we never do."

Theresa: "I want to be able to have a friend spend the night and go out with my new boyfriend . . . he doesn't do drugs."

Mom: "He is nice. . ."

LM: "When you return, then, next week and you have begun to accomplish just a little of what you have told me were your goals, Dad, what do you think you might tell me was different?"

Dad: "I think if she wants to go somewhere, we need to know with whom and where she is going. I will make a contract with her for no drugs on that evening. Maybe one weekday night and one weekend date. I realize now that when we are very restrictive, she cooperates . . . like with the smoking."

Mom: "I think she needs other activities and I want the grades to improve drastically."

Theresa: "I want them to trust me more."

LM: "I wonder what might encourage that to happen?"

Theresa: "I suppose I could cut down on the marijuana."

The family left and returned two weeks later. Theresa had kept her bargain and was given small privileges with her friends. After a month passed, Theresa and her family returned and I barely recognized Theresa. The black eyeliner and lipstick were gone and, instead of baggy clothes, she sported an outfit she had sewn. Her mother glowed as she relayed the times she and her daughter spent at the fabric store. Theresa had been taking home economics that semester and fell in love with sewing. When she had smoked pot, she was often too tired to do her project. With less of the substance influencing her, she was beginning to enjoy sewing. Her goal was now to be a fashion designer and model. Her mom had made an appointment at a local modeling agency and reported that she and her daughter were becoming close again. The change in Theresa was phenomenal. Her father reported that each evening she left to go with friends, he met the friends, and made a contract with Theresa. She referred to them as lectures. Her father said he would continue lecturing until the drug screen was clean. She was due for the second screen in a week.

The important interventions of this case occurred in the parents' ability to:

a. redirect their daughter towards other interests

b. restrict friends whom they felt were bad influences on her

c. give out small privileges for small changes

d. expect small improvements with a long-term expectation of their daughter to become drug free

While they initially would have liked their daughter to give up all drug use, the daughter's rebellion against that made it less likely to occur. However, by creating an environment in which the daughter could see small rewards from small gains, *and* in which she knew she was being supervised, the family gathered together against the habit. Eventually Theresa became drug free, brought up all of her grades, and was given the opportunity to attend a new high school in the fall. Her father continued the lectures!

Concluding Comments

To paraphrase David Epson, a therapist and author from New Zealand, "People get stuck trying to fit their stories into new stories that do not fit." This feeling of "stuckness" contributes to many of the crises people have. This chapter has asked you to cooperate with the feelings and events that often take over children and adolescents, producing crises in their lives. The chapter asks you to suspend your beliefs about what they **need** to do and to look at what works with them.

Notice how all of the interventions are similar:

1. *The parents figured out what worked with their kids by planning and thinking prior to the intervention. They started small and expected more as successes grew.*

2. *Prior to the crisis, the parents created an atmosphere of cooperation and respect. They didn't wait for a crisis to occur before they talked to their kids.*

3. *The parents took time to understand the "context" of the event and took action immediately.*

4. *They validated who their kids were and did not associate the kids with the "badness" of the event occurring. They tried to see them as separate and assisted them in continuing to separate them from the problem.*

5. *The parents gave their kids opportunities to be successful and watched for those successes to give them privileges back and to give their kids the idea that **the kids** solved the problem.*

"Making music is another way of making children."

—*Friedrich Nietzsche*

Chapter
8

Preparing for the Launch

**Transitions from Adult to New Parent . . .
Child to Adult . . . Parent to Grandparent . . .**

"We are shaped and fashioned by what we love."

—*Johann Wolfgang von Goethe*

T ransitions and change are part of life, yet many of us rebel when faced with a change that threatens our familiar roles. We like things the way they are. We know our place, our routine, and our purpose. When life transitions happen and a new person enters into the world, the lives of more than just *the couple* change drastically. Now, parents become grandparents, adults become parents, and a child becomes the center of everyone's world.

The beauty of the generational ties that bind also becomes tested as persons scamper around, trying to understand where they *fit*. Sometimes the *fit* is so uncomfortable, the old roles try to remain . . . but leave it to change to take over and force the issue eventually.

Within the generations of old and new lie the stories of the future. As an eighteen-year-old launches his way into a college dorm, a twenty-four-year-old has her first baby, and the fifty-year-old touches his first granddaughter, new stories emerge that will designate the roles of family members . . . until the next change occurs. This chapter will attempt to offer ideas to make the transitions of life easier. While there will still be bumps to jar oneself and cracks to fall into for a while, the road continues on, never-ending and always interesting. Read now about how focusing on *how you dealt with change* before may help you now.

On Becoming New Parents

When the young married couple had reached the age of twenty-five, they began having their children. They planned their family with the skill of mapmakers, still enjoying themselves as inseparable lovers who adored each moment they were together. They were girlfriend and boyfriend, best friends and pals, confidants and sounding boards. The world seemed to fade away when they were together. Then the children arrived.

Over the years he changed from husband to "Dad" and she changed from wife to "Mom," and the children were reared with love and joy and all of the comforts of a family destined to thrive. But the couple became lost. Years later, after the divorce, she sat in a counselor's office describing to the "paid sounding board" that she realized now how great a father he was and how poor a wife she had been. Enamored with her babies she had forgotten that she had been his best friend once. As she kept up with the household and chauffeured the kids to soccer and dancing lessons, she forgot to keep up with him. She passed the movie theater that they had not been to for years without noticing. She didn't see the restaurant where they celebrated their third anniversary as she passed it on the way to work. Today in the counselor's office, married to the second husband, she is noticing and wishing she had paid attention to him as much as she paid attention to the kids. (This story was relayed to me by Stephen Chilton, M.S., 1996.)

The road to parenthood is filled with trials and tribulations of parenting, but it is also filled with cracks in which one's couplehood can be lost. In my work as a family therapist I hear similar stories from couples who search for what they once had. As desires change and time diminishes, couples turn into individuals fighting a clock of responsibility that never ends. There had always been time before and now it is scarcely noticed if a conversation is never complete.

Yet there is a need in a new parent's life to be loved, respected, and assisted by the partner *in the same way they began as a couple* and if it does not occur when parenthood begins, the needs are met by the child. Children adore their mother and father . . . they smile and coo and give love back to the caregiver who gives them life. Without an adult to give the same, the child becomes a substitute.

One of the dearest professors who taught a family therapy class to me years ago was once asked about how parents should teach kids about love. He replied:

> *"The best way in the world to teach kids about relationships is to have Mom and Dad hug each other, kiss each other and be caught making out in front of the kids!"*

Think about it. What do your kids do when you kiss your spouse? Notice next time. Most couples whom I ask to notice their kids' responses report that their kids become happy, giggling, and carrying on with smiles on their faces. Of course they love seeing their parents love each other because it makes them feel so *safe*. There is no greater gift besides love that we can give our kids than to give them the emotional safety of knowing they are cared for by people who care about each other. How, then, can you convey to your kids that all is well on the homefront? By becoming a couple . . . again!

Reclaim Your Couplehood by Reclaiming Yourself First

Michelle Weiner-Davis, author of *Divorce Busting, A Revolutionary and Rapid Program for Staying Together,* mentions in the following quotation from her book how important it is for parents to maintain time for themselves in order to be the best parents possible:

> *"If you think about it objectively for a moment, when you are burned out you cannot really be available to your children. You have*

nothing left to give. Furthermore, since you know that children learn by example, if you take charge of your life and feel good about your-self, you are setting an example for your children to follow in their own lives. If instead you continually make sacrifices to spend time with your children, you are bound to feel resentment, which will be reflected in your interactions with them. Taking even a small breather can go a long way toward restoring a positive outlook or peace of mind" (Weiner-Davis, 1992, pp. 195–196).

Even though you are now a parent with new responsibilities, still take an occasional moment to recall how you fought stress in the past. While bringing a new human being into the world is quite different from last year's work-related presentation, the preparation, patience, and determination to succeed is the same. So is the manner in which you calmed yourself down when you were under stressful situations.

For example, attempt to keep your sanity with a modified exercise routine or dressing schedule, slightly similar to the ones you kept before the children came. A new mom once came to talk to me because she was depressed over the lack of time she had after having her two children, ages one and two. She brought with her a photo of herself before the children: slim, polished, hair and makeup meticulously done. Now, before me was a fatigued and frail woman who took no time for herself each week. Somewhere among the trips to the grocery store, pediatrician, and diaper pail, she had lost herself. She and I spent our hour brainstorming how she was able to keep a clean home and work forty hours a week three years ago. She told me of her methods of organization at work and home during those days and within a few minutes, decided upon a plan for her next week. When she realized that she basically needed only a total of two hours a week (out of 168 hours per week) to feel more polished, she decided to do one less chore per morning in exchange for a higher priority . . . herself. Not only did her self-esteem improve within two weeks, so did her marriage.

After reclaiming yourself, take a few minutes per week to do things you used to do as a couple. Sure, things are different, time is more scarce, conversations rarely get completed, but you were a couple first. The questions on the following pages are designed to help you recall and perhaps rekindle some sparkle in your relationship. Do these with your partner while the kids sleep!

Ideas for Getting Back in Touch With Each Other

1. *Go back in time for a moment and recall what you were first attracted to in your partner. Ask your partner to tell you the same. List those attractive traits below.*

_____

_____

2. *List the activities you both enjoyed doing together when your relationship started. List also what those activities did for you as a couple.*

_____

_____

3. *What did your partner do more of before that made you feel more respected, loved, and important to him/her? Ask your partner what you did before that gave him/her that same satisfaction.*

_____

_____

4. *While your life has changed and some of the memorable activities may be difficult to recreate, how could you begin to repeat them on a small scale?*

_____

_____

5. *At your work, or home with the kids, you probably have to schedule in important tasks such as laundry, cooking, working, scheduling daycare, etc. How do you do this? How do you make time for these important events?*

_____

_____

6. *If you were to take your answers from #5 and schedule in your answers from #3 and #4, what might you and your partner begin to do just for a week to get closer to each other again?*

_____

_____

What could your partner do specially that would help this to happen for you?

_____

What would your partner say you could do to help this happen for him/her?

_____

7. *On a scale of 1 to 10, with 10 = total couplehood and 1 = little to no couplehood, where are you at this moment on the scale below? Where would you like to be by next week?*

> no couplehood_____couplehood
> 1   2   3   4   5   6   7   8   9   10

8. *What are your current beliefs or expectations about your partner?*

_____

_____

What might happen if you changed your beliefs and expectations just slightly during the next week? (This question was suggested by Stephen Chilton, M.S.)

_____

_____

_____

_____

Raising Them from Children to Adults

Writing this book has been good *medicine* for me. During the year of manuscript proposal and then completion, my older son, Roger Jr., learned to drive and then gained his driver's license. As I waited up for him each evening upon his return from working at our local baseball stadium, I often took a break from the book and drifted off recalling other moments of *history* that he created:

- riding a bike
- going to kindergarten the first day
- attending the first school dance
- installing the first loud stereo
- driving off in his first car
- his first job

Tough experiences but wonderful memories have been made during his brief history on earth . . . all within the link of human development. Thinking about his departure to college in two years makes me sad and happy at the same time . . . sad to see him go but happy to see him enter a new realm of life. Recently, a friend whose kids played with mine in the sandbox many years ago told me about the many trials and tribulations of his son's last two years. As he was accepted into college after graduation, his dad at first was depressed over his son's nearing departure. I casually mentioned how much easier things were when the kids were younger. He then looked at me and said:

> *"I don't think so . . . I'm happy that he's gotten to this point. Sure, it's been tough at times, yet I can now look forward with him to all of the things he can experience in college next year. Letting go seems easier when I think of it in this way."*

In the same way that your child grows from a toddler to an adolescent, and then into an adult leaving home, so should your parenting skills grow and evolve with him/her. As you modify your ways of loving your kids, do not forget that they probably still treasure the way you talked to them, did kind things for them, and were *there* for them. As he/she matures, watch also for the clues given as to *how* to let go more painlessly:

a. Notice the times when it is easier for your young adult to talk to you . . . and respect those times and your young adult's private life.

b. Notice his/her goals for the future and support them, even if they don't match yours. Remember, goals change as experience occurs. Your expressed belief in his/her decisions without too much advice will be appreciated.

c. Utilize the ways you nurtured him/her in the past in a grown-up manner. Chances are the ways you talked, cared, and helped in the past will still be appreciated. Just because he is 6'3" doesn't mean he stopped loving your chocolate chip cookies.

d. When he/she shows more distance, instead of thinking about it as isolating from the family, see it as "individuating," a fancy word that means "growing into an individual." Respect his/her individuality and desire to be grown up.

e. Realize the need for him/her to be responsible and recall ways during his/her childrearing in which you helped that to occur, even with small tasks. Take the time to mention these even now when he/she is responsible, and attempt to recognize how you might have helped that to happen.

f. Look at his/her new relationships as the beginning of a new genogram, and that your methods of parenting helped to produce what may happen in the future. Remember, without actually realizing it, he/she will formulate a family legacy for himself/herself. Give your best performance!

Exploring the Future

As a final exercise for thinking about the transition from child to adult, read the caption below and process it with your partner using the guiding questions afterwards.

It is twenty years in the future. Your children are grown, married, or are in relationships. They are raising their own children as you peek in on them one day. Their children are still young and the days are hectic. One day a reporter, wandering around doing research on family life, interviews your son or daughter about childhood experiences. On the lines below, fill in what you hope your son or daughter might answer.

1. *What were the beliefs of your parents about you as a person?*

_____

_____

2. *How did your parents deal with conflict between themselves or with you?*

_____

_____

3. *How did your parents view themselves as a couple?*

_____

_____

4. *What were the basic family values you learned while growing up? How do you think you learned them?*

_____

_____

_____

5. *If you packed a family suitcase of the favorite qualities of your parents and their beliefs, what would you pack and give to your children today?*

_____

_____

_____

How will you assist your child/adolescent in carrying on the answers you just considered? Each day is an opportunity to express or demonstrate your wishes for their family legacy. Every trial and conflict handled effectively teaches lessons for life. Never miss a coincidence or a chance to convey strategies or ways to live life to its fullest, even when life gets tough. Tell them what you feel is appropriate information (but never so much that it causes them to worry) and then share with them how you worked through your problems as well. This will strengthen their belief in you and widen their knowledge of strategies for their future.

From Your Parents to Grandparents. . . Gathering Knowledge from an Experienced Generation

In a bookstore recently, I picked up several books written for grandparents describing "how to be a great grandparent." Out of all of the books, one statement caught my eye: **"Teach them about bugs."**

The reason I enjoyed this silly statement so much was because of its ultimate simplicity. The glamour of grandparenthood seems to lie in the ability of an experienced generation to explain, with plenty of patience, all of the intricate details of topics that parents sometimes forget to explain. For example:

- How do they make chocolate chips?
- How do they make popsicles?
- Why do birds all fly together in one direction?
- How does snow stick together?
- Why are pickles called 'pickles'?

In the same way, consider also, as you rear your own new family, that you are creating a new relationship with your child's grandparents and relationships require nurturing. Attempt to not cut off well-meant advice; instead, attempt to see it as a *sharing of experiences*. The following questions may be helpful as you evolve into a separate family, yet still connected with your family of *origin*.

Guiding Questions for New Parents to Think About

1. *How do we as a couple want things to be in our new family?*

   _____

   _____

2. *Is there a conflict between our beliefs in childrearing and our parents' beliefs? If so, what are the similarities we share? How could concentrating on our similarities lessen conflict?*

   _____

_____

3. *How do we typically deal with differences in opinion with other people? Would these strategies be suitable to try with our parents when we differ on certain issues?*

_____

_____

_____

4. *If we redescribed our parents' worries, concerns, advice-giving, and helpfulness as assistance and good will, would it change the way we interact with them? In what way?*

_____

_____

_____

5. *How could we begin on a small scale to set the stage for how we want our relationship to be in the near future? What personal skills from other areas could we use to accomplish this?*

_____

_____

_____

Concluding Comments

It seems fitting to end this book with a quote from one of my favorite books, *The Celestine Prophecy*, written by James Redfield. In his book, Redfield wrote so wisely of the coincidences of life and the importance of paying attention to them. As I wrote this book, opportunities for conversations with my family, friends, and colleagues emerged that enriched the book's content and widened my scope of parenting. While I am the author, the encounters provided the sketchpad for developing the ideas you have in your hand. Without those persons who crossed *my path,* there would be no book. Mr. Redfield wrote:

> "... *whenever people cross our paths, there is always a message for us. Chance encounters do not exist. But how we respond to these encounters determines whether we're able to receive the message. If we have a conversation with someone who crosses our path and we do not see a message pertaining to our current questions, it does not mean there was no message. It only means we missed it for some reason"* (1993, p. 200).

As you lay down this book today, pay attention to how your children cross your path, how your partner crosses it with you, and how those who watch on the sidelines influence your steps. Watch for the effective ways of loving your kids. Those new solutions will change *their* pathways for the better.

Stories of Exceptional Families from Around the World

"Sometimes I think we're alone in the universe, and sometimes
I think we're not. In either case, the idea is quite staggering."

—Arthur C. Clarke

T his unique Appendix is composed of several stories of families, gra-
ciously shared with me by friends I have met through doing workshops
and professional encounters. When I went *looking* for cases to fill this
Appendix, these persons enthusiastically not only gave me permission to
use their work, but impressed me by their continual desire to learn more.
What will be unique in this Appendix are the thoughts of the therapists I
will include, allowing you to read the stories through a therapist's eyes. I
hope you will enjoy the stories that follow and notice the similar focus on
solutions, instead of problems.

"Treating The House Like a Hotel: From Simile to Metaphor" —Brian Cade, Private Practice, Sydney, Australia* (excerpts reprinted with permission)

Most if not all of us will have come across parents who, talking of their teenager, complain that he or she "treats the house just like a hotel." The following case study is one out of a number of extreme situations in which parents have been persuaded to take the metaphor of their house-as-hotel to its logical conclusion.

The Family

Lianne was a fifteen-year-old young woman who could easily be taken for eighteen years old or more. She was brought to me by her mother and stepfather. They described her as being totally beyond their control. She had rarely attended school over the previous two years. She typically spent three or four days at a time away from home, living, as far as they knew, either with whoever was her current boyfriend or with various friends. Sometimes she would stay away for weeks at a time, usually after a major argument with one or both of them. When crossed or in the face of either of them attempting to reason with her about any aspect of her lifestyle, she would often become verbally abusive. On several occasions, she had physically attacked her mother.

As they described the situation to me, Lianne sat with a bored or defiant look on her face. She declined to comment when invited either by me or by them to do so, just shrugging her shoulders and reminding her parents that they were the ones who had wanted to come and see me. She had nothing to say.

It is usually my policy with escalating parent/adolescent problems, after a brief family interview that allows me to develop a sense of how the members operate together, to split the two generations up, seeing the adolescent first and then the parents. As I have pointed out elsewhere,

---

*This article was published in its entirety in *Case Studies in Brief and Family Therapy,* 1994, 8(1), 5-14. For journal information, contact Michael Durrant, P.O. Box 630, Epping, NSW, Australia, 2121.

". . . The more the parents attempt to control, protect, help or guide the adolescent, the more the adolescent is driven to retreat or rebel. The more the adolescent tries to 'find space' by avoiding, by arguing with, or by disobeying their 'over-intrusive' parents (as they see them), the more they confirm their parents' doubts and fears and thus attract further attention from them." (Cade, 1988, p. 31)

The session with Lianne was easier than I had expected. She said she didn't mind talking to me though she couldn't see how it would make any difference. She had no intentions of changing her lifestyle. She was clearly giving away as little as possible and I decided not to ask anything about this lifestyle. However, she did respond to the question:

BC: "If you were me, what would you want to advise your parents to do, assuming they would listen to me?"

She admitted that her stepfather's "interminable sermons" and her mother's "slimy, underhand attempts at getting close to me" were driving her crazy. She was clearly not a customer for anything from me at this point, but did infer that, if I could find a way of getting them off her back, she would probably end up giving them less of a hard time.

Lianne: "But I'd have to be sure it was for good. Who wants to hang around to be lectured or slobbered over?"

She admitted that they probably did have some cause to be concerned about her but said that it was her life and that she knew exactly what she was doing. I said that I would see what I could do about getting them off her back but I couldn't promise anything; and I didn't think I could stop them from worrying about her.

Lianne: "That's O.K., as long as they keep it to themselves."

John, her stepfather was a kind though somewhat (in his own words) old-fashioned man. Born of a Dutch farmer and an English mother, and brought up in Holland, he was of the view that children had to learn right from wrong, and that Lianne had to learn to obey their rules. Widely read, he was familiar with the rational emotive approach to therapy and had been attempting to apply the ideas with his stepdaughter, to no avail. He was a great believer in the power of logic and of rational argument but was prone to giving long lectures (at one point in a later session he admitted that he was "perhaps not so good at the listening side of debating").

Sally, the mother, an English teacher, was Australian. She had divorced her first husband, Lianne's and younger daughter Jennifer's natural father, because of his drinking and the increasing extent of his violence. For a few years, she and the two girls had lived alone together until she met and married John when Lianne was eleven. There had initially been no apparent tension in the relationship between stepfather and stepdaughter (although they had been expecting it).

The problems had started after they had been contacted by Lianne's school a couple of years earlier and informed that she had been truant regularly. As far as they had been aware, she had been attending regularly. She had been both leaving for school and arriving back home at the appropriate time. It became clear she had been using a friend's house for changing out of and, later in the day, changing back into her school uniform. From then on the situation had deteriorated. Lianne gave up any pretense of cooperation and became increasingly defiant. A short period living with her natural father (at her request) had been a near disaster. They had been permanently "at daggers drawn." According to John, Lianne and her natural father were too much alike in temperament. Following her return, things had continued to become worse and worse.

She was regularly using drugs and alcohol. They feared she had probably been financing the drug habit through occasional periods of prostitution. She had also stolen valuable items of jewelry and porcelain from them, although she had denied this. Not wishing to alienate her further, they had not informed the police about the thefts. After the periods away, she would return home and:

- sleep more-or-less continuously for a couple of days
- eat prodigious amounts of food
- demand that her mother wash her clothes
- disappear again

At other times, she might stay with them for several weeks; usually "on her own terms." Sometimes, at such times, John would try to renegotiate some basic ground rules and, in the face of John's further attempts to discuss the situation "rationally" with her, she would storm out. John never threatened her nor struck her; he did not agree with violence as an answer to any problem. She would treat any appeal from her mother with contempt. Yet, at times, she would suddenly and spontaneously hug her mother.

Mom: ". . . as though with desperation as though she was aching to beg my forgiveness. Yet, if it was contrition, it never succeeded in breaking through that hard outer shell. It breaks my heart to catch such a brief glimpse of that lonely child and then to see her shoulders stiffening, and her face hardening all over again."

The younger sister, Jennifer, also often felt the brunt of Lianne's temper. Aged thirteen, she was doing well in school. Her parents described her as "tractable" and "sweet natured." They described how they often felt it necessary to protect her from her older sister's scorn and anger and occasional physical attacks. They were aware, however, that this probably served, in the end, only further to fuel Lianne's frustration and fury. But they did not know what else to do. Sally tended to defer to her husband's opinion, though clearly she did not always agree with his stricter demands of Lianne. She was aware that she would tend to give way "for the sake of peace." However, there was really not a high level of disagreement between them about either the unacceptableness of her behavior or the general standards to which they wished her to conform.

Some Validation and Passing on of Experience

I pointed out to them that, in my opinion, this was perhaps the most difficult era in which to bring up children, even though a Babylonian tablet had been discovered, which must be about 3,000 to 4,000 years old, on which had been inscribed,

> *Today's youth is rotten to the core; it is evil, Godless and lazy. It will never be what youth used to be, and it will never be able to preserve our culture. (referred to in Watzlawick, 1974, p. 33)*

We also looked at the problems that stem from there being no clear rite of passage to demark the move from the status of child to the status of adult. When should they be considered grown up? Is it at puberty, when nature decides they are old enough to reproduce? Is it when they leave school? Is it when they reach sixteen and are legally allowed to make their own decisions about leaving home and about sex? Is it when they can have a driver's license? Is it when they are old enough to join the army and die for their country? Is it when they leave home? Is it when they are twenty-one, the once traditional age for receiving the key of the door?

In terms of the problems between Lianne and Jennifer, we looked at how easy it is for a parent to take on the role of trying to keep the peace or to protect one child from the other. On an occasional basis, this is unlikely to be a problem. However, if it begins to become a position that a parent feels constantly forced to take, then it is time to consider what is happening and whether the approaches being used are working or, as they had already become concerned about, are they inadvertently adding fuel to the situation.

Whatever the rights and wrongs of the situation as far as either parent is concerned, once they were seen to take sides, they inevitably ended up with an aggrieved daughter who felt that an injustice had been done. The righteous indignation accompanying this sense of injustice led to her being determined to right the wrong at the earliest possible opportunity, usually by doing something to hit back either at them or at Jennifer (who was clearly often seen as being to blame by being such a "slimy goody goody").

I commiserated with how, as a parent, it can often be hard to stand back in the face of siblings fighting, particularly when it is feared that one may be hurt. Yet, in the long run, siblings must largely be left to sort out their differences themselves. The more parents intervene, the less likely it will be that they will learn to do this, and the more the parent(s) could be drawn into an endless cycle. Lianne will have become adept at knowing just which strings to pull to get the parent(s) involved in yet another fruitless battle. Neither, I suspected, would Jennifer always be totally innocent, however convincingly she appeared to be so. They agreed with this and were able to describe examples of Jennifer having seemed deliberately to have goaded her sister into a rage. Lianne will believe they are always picking on her and at her, and she will be oblivious to the contributions she is making to this process (and it will usually be totally use-less, even inflammatory, to point this fact out to her). Underneath the tough surface, troubled and troublesome adolescents often loath themselves and what they are doing (though they would be highly unlikely to admit this, particularly to their parents). They very much agreed that this was probably the case with Lianne.

The Seed of an Idea

The difficulty with dealing with such situations once they have become deeply entrenched is that Lianne probably needs them to be proactive in spending time with her, showing an interest in her, lov-ing her unconditionally, responding positively, but at *their own* insti-gation rather than for the sake of peace or as a result of her wearing them down. This can be extremely difficult once demoralization, weariness, and resentment have set in. She would be also unlikely, at first, to trust any changes in responses and would be likely to test the situation, usually by increasing the behaviors that tended in the past to "pull their strings." Outlasting this phase can be tough.

Mom and Dad: "But it's difficult to know where to start. She's hardly around for us to even begin to try some of these ideas out. She's basically using our house just like a hotel."

I realized that in this simile was the seed of an idea that might help them through this phase.

BC: "I think you might have a potential answer there."

We began to look together at how a hotel treats an occasional but regular guest. The parents were quickly drawn enthusiastically into an elaboration of the following ideas.

We agreed that, for a start, hotel staff do not immediately bom-bard you with questions such as,

"Where have you been?"

"Who have you been with?"

"Don't you know how worried we have been about you?"

"Look at the state of you. Haven't you been eating properly?"

"Can't you see how you're throwing your life away?"

They are more likely to approach you in a welcoming though not overwhelming fashion.

"It's good to see you again."

"Your room is ready for you."

"There are clean towels laid out if you would like a shower."

"Would you like a cup of tea or coffee?"

"Dinner will be at eight. Will you be eating with us?"

"Do you have any laundry that needs to be done?"

"Is there anything else you would like?"

They respect your privacy and demand nothing of you by way of specific activities nor ask about your plans for the future. If a guest is troublesome, the staff will show considerable tolerance to a wide range of behaviors. Only if the guest becomes too noisy, abusive, or threatening will they begin to react, initially responding politely though increasingly firmly, asking them quietly to desist. They may finally politely ask the person to leave and, as a final response, call the police to have them ejected.

When, after your stay, you finally go, the staff do not bombard you with questions such as,

"Where are you going then?"

"When are you coming back?"

"What about school?"

They usually wish you all the best.

"It was nice to see you again. We hope you had a good stay. We look forward to seeing you the next time you are passing through this way."

The Process of Persuasion

Central to the parents being prepared to try out this idea was their complete acceptance that everything they had been trying so far had not worked and was unlikely to have any effect were they to continue trying the same approaches in the future. If either of the parents had felt that their approach might finally work, or had been hooked into the stubborn position that it was Lianne who *had* to learn, *had* to change, then it would not have been appropriate to proceed with the suggestion. It is not always easy to feel that *not* doing something, that backing away from an escalation, can actually be *doing something positive.* Parents can easily feel they are giving up, or it is *they* who are having to make all of the concessions. Again, if this had been an issue for these parents, this approach would unlikely have been productive. To this end, I gave them a copy of "Approaches that Usually Do Not Work" (see Chapter 3), a handout I often share with people to help them work out what it is that they might inadvertently be doing that has become fruitless—however correct, logical, or justifiable it seems to be.

I highlighted how important it was not to take responsibility for areas of an adolescent's life over which, in the end, you basically have little or no control, areas in which, eventually, they must find their own way. Unfortunately, some of these areas are those that can give parents the greatest cause for concern, such as the way they deal with school, their choice of friends, their attitudes towards and about sex, alcohol, drugs, etc. It is a sad fact that a parent's unsolicited advice, guidance, or attempts to protect or to control in any of these areas can often have the very opposite outcome to the one being sought. However, it is important that parents be there for the adolescents to turn to when they need help and support; that they feel safe they can do this without meeting rejection or a barrage of criticisms such as, "I told you so. You have made your own bed and now you must lie on it!" or "It's your own fault!"

We discussed the problem that the more rules you have, the more likely they are to be broken, particularly if many of them are over what the adolescent sees as relatively trivial things. Long lists of negative comments or complaints tend to produce instant deafness or defiance. We also looked at the importance of avoiding becoming a permanent Sherlock Holmes, constantly hunting for evidence of lies and deceit. The position "I will not trust you until you prove that you can be trusted" invariably worsens a situation. Adolescents tend just to get better and better at lying or deceiving or end up just not caring whether you believe them or not. Parents have to trust and have that trust broken, trust and have that trust broken, trust and have that trust broken—endlessly, hard, and sometimes frightening though that position can be to maintain. Paradoxically, it is a position that is much more likely to work in the long run.

The Following Sessions

At the next session, the parents reported that, though Lianne had not changed her lifestyle, she had been "much less objectionable." They had been able to avoid many of the "approaches that usually do not work" (in fact, they asked for a new copy because the original copy I had given them was now covered with notes), though it had by no means been easy, particularly when, on one occasion, Lianne had arrived home drunk. They found the metaphor of the hotel extremely helpful. When in doubt about how to react, they discovered that they were usually able, by discussing how hotel staff faced with similar circumstances might react, to find a way of responding to Lianne that avoided an escalation but left them feeling empowered. They found that doing nothing could actually feel like doing something.

The next few sessions were essentially devoted to my encouraging them to persevere in the direction that was clearly, slowly beginning to have an effect. There was no miracle cure. Lianne did not suddenly turn into an amenable, cooperative daughter. However, she began to talk to her mother about wanting to start sorting out the mess that her life was in. She also talked of returning to school and working towards her High School Certificate. The parents rapidly found that, if they became too enthusiastic about these intentions and therefore too helpful, Lianne would begin struggling with *them* rather than with the problems. They learned to respond encouragingly but more cautiously, taking a position such as,

Mom and Dad: "That sounds like a good idea. We hope it sorts out for you. Let us know if we can be of any help."

Several months later, quite out of the blue, Lianne telephoned and asked to see me. She was concerned with the way she was being exploited financially, emotionally, and sexually by her current boyfriend. I saw her for a couple of sessions. She described how she hated herself. We looked in detail at how specifically she would be different as she began to accept and respect herself more and to find more and more ways of not being so easily exploited. She canceled the third session because she had found a part time job, but let me know that she had ended the relationship with her boyfriend. He had been angry and had threatened her, but she had "stuck to her guns" (one of the ways she had said that she would be different as she began to respect herself more).

My last contact was with the mother, about one year later. Lianne was studying for her High School Certificate. She was still doing drugs, but far less frequently. She still stayed out all night on occasions, but not for days at a time and usually she would let her parents know. She was still a very private person, but the parents no longer experienced the abusive and violent explosions that used to occur. There were times when she would talk much more openly to her mother. She was more physically demonstrative, even to her stepfather with whom she would also sometimes enjoy "a logical debate about some issue or other." They did not think she had ever worked as a prostitute again and, although she currently did not have a steady boyfriend, she appeared not to be behaving so promiscuously anymore. She felt they still had a long way to go, but both she and John felt they could now weather whatever storms might still be ahead.

Mom and Dad: "We still occasionally ask ourselves 'how would an experience hotelier deal with this'?"

"Five Superstars"
—Michael Bishop, Ph.D., Private Practice, Arlington, Texas*

The Family

The Nova family sat in the waiting room. They had called for a counseling appointment because their youngest child, Billy, age 10, was having difficulty in school. One of his teachers had suggested that he had ADHD (attention deficit hyperactivity disorder). The family was also concerned. They described him as "disruptive" and always getting into trouble.

The Nova family consisted of Dad, a prominent physician whose patients were among the wealthiest and most influential in the city. He was tall, athletic, handsome and articulate. Mom was as attractive as a runway model. She was well educated and was currently busy making travel plans for her upcoming promotional tour of her latest publication. Their older son, Robert, age 17, was a National Merit Quarterfinalist, who was trying to decide which private college tennis scholarship to accept. Cindy, their daughter, was a pretty, blonde fourteen-year-old who was a starter on her basketball, softball, and soccer teams. Up until a few weeks ago, Billy and Cindy were in a constant state of picking and arguing that often resulted in pushing and shoving. Billy was an active, pudgy ten-year-old who was exploring the corners of the waiting room while the other four members of his family were reading their magazines quietly. They looked up occasionally, only to correct Billy's wanderings. Billy, after all, was the reason they were there.

In addition to quarrels with his sister, recently the tension switched to Billy and his brother Robert with an increase in physical confrontations. The question the parents had come to the session with was:

Mom and Dad: "Should we put Billy on medication for ADHD?"

After spending a few minutes with the entire family, most of which was used to describe the chaos in the family because of Billy's behavior, I stopped the session and visited with Billy alone. Billy described a feeling of frustration at "being a problem" and didn't

---

Michael Bishop, Ph.D. focuses on the "experiential" side of therapy in his work as a family therapist.

know why things were so hard and did not work out for him. I had a sense of this youngster being lost in the stars and not knowing where his place was in his family.

I brought the entire family back into my office and asked them if they were adventurers who would like to experience a type of therapy activity that might be a little different. Being a family that "eats challenging competitions for breakfast," they agreed to the different activity if it would be helpful for Billy and their family. After ten minutes of juggling three Day Runners, one personal calendar, and a therapist's appointment book, we found a time to meet during the following week.

The Tent, the Video Camera, and Too Many Chiefs!

When the next appointment arrived, I brought the family into a large group room containing six chairs and a video camera, already set up. I threw a navy bag two feet long and fourteen inches in diameter into the middle of the room.

MB: "Your assignment is to assemble this good enough for you to use."

Cindy: "What is it?"

Billy: "I know!"

Mom: "Is it a tent?"

Billy: "Yea, it's like the one we used at my friend's house."

Dad and Robert began pulling the parts out of the bag . . .

Billy: "Those are the poles!"

Robert: "Here, Billy. Go over there and put these together." (Robert handed the ten sections of tent poles to Billy.)

The rest of the family did not acknowledge Billy's previous experience with this type of tent. Instead, they began taking an inventory of the parts to the tent which included two large bundles of tent material. They started to spread the smaller piece on the ground as a floor.

Billy: "No, ya'll. That's the top!" (He completes the first of two long tent poles.)

Mom: "Maybe we should read the instructions." (She soon discovers the printed assembly instructions.)

Mom then proceeded to read the instructions as Robert and Dad turn the tent materials in various positions.

Billy: "These go in the loops over here." (He completes a second pole and swings it into Mom's face, which soon changes to an angry expression as she continues to read the directions.)

Mom: "Billy, please be careful!"

The family continues to make progress on their task with Billy making suggestions that are instantly ignored.

The tent nears completion, with only the top "rain fly" needing an adjustment. Billy enters the tent to inspect it from the inside. He gives instructions, correctly describing how the rain fly should be positioned. The rest of the family seems satisfied with the structure except for Mom. She continues to study the tent and the printed instructions while Billy enjoys the view from the inside. The rest of the family watches Mom.

Robert: "Mom, your problem is that you've built something that is not perfect." (He bends down and looks at her face to face from a distance of about twelve inches.)

Mom: "That's not the point. It's a kit that should all fit together." (She looks at me.) "We've got too many chiefs and no Indians in this group!"

The family completed the task to everyone's satisfaction in about twenty minutes. I asked the family to gather into a circle to discuss their experience of the activity. They came up with the following themes that they seemed to enjoy:

- having fun
- getting a sense of accomplishment
- cooperation and teamwork

Mom: "I got frustrated because it didn't all fit together. It drives me crazy when things aren't complete. I guess I need closure."

The discussion soon turned to Billy as he started being active in his chair. The family moved from talking about his behavior in the chair to his behavior at home.

Billy: "I'm the bad person in the family."

The discussion quickly focused on "What we do and what should we do when Billy is bad."

I began discussing Billy, but from the point of view of him being the *expert* in the family in many ways, but especially during the activity of the tent assembly. At first, the family was surprised to hear this description. I began to point out the *correct instructions* he had given the family during the activity. They did not seem to have a memory of those instructions. Because of time, I took the parents into another room while the three children began to watch the playback of the video we had made. While with the parents, I discussed with them the idea of trying a small dose of medication to help Billy focus only during school for a short time, under the direction of a physician other than Dad. We also discussed how being the youngest member of a family of "superstars" might mean he needs more and more encouragement. I mentioned that he seemed to have a lot to live up to in such a fast-paced, active, and successful household.

Mom was not convinced that the family had ignored Billy's suggestions about assembling the tent. We returned to the other room where the children were watching the video that was showing the family about halfway through the exercise of building the tent.

Cindy: "Billy really did know how to do this and none of us listened to him."

At this point, Billy wanted to have all of us watch the entire video even though we were twenty minutes past our session time. We replayed about six minutes of the activity in which we captured many of Billy's helpful suggestions and the reactions of his family towards him. Mom was holding Billy close to her when she commented that she did not realize how she had ignored him.

We ended the session with my declaration that they were a fortunate family to have FIVE superstar experts in the family. I said that so many families only have one or *none*. I asked the family to call if they needed another session.

Follow Up

I did not hear from the family for four months. I decided to call them and follow up on their family's progress. Talking to Dad, he stated that they had gone to their official family physician and started Billy on a very small dose of medication for hyperactivity. Billy was doing very well in school now and things were going well for him and everyone in the family.

Was this a *different* activity? Yes. Did the activity create a change or was it the small amount of medication? Who knows. The important thing that seemed to develop was that the Nova family began to see Billy as successful, probably creating an environment that convinced Billy he was. He responded positively at school where he took the medication, yet continued to develop a positive, healthy relationship at *home* without it.

"How's the Weather Today? A Case of School Refusal" —Larry Furmanczyk, M.A., School Social Worker, Prince George, British Columbia

The Situation

The principal referred this case of "school refusal" to me. He perceived that the parents were being cooperative with the school yet were wavering in giving in to their nine-year-old daughter's demands to be taken home from school each day. She would cling to her mother and scream. Later, physical complaints developed that resulted in her not attending school at all. After about seven weeks of persistent attempts (including coercion, threats, bargaining, etc.), the girl would not sleep at night nor get up in the morning. She was depressed and expressing suicidal ideation. She wasn't smiling or playing in her usual manner.

The First Session

At first, I briefly met with the girl's teacher and principal to do an assessment. I was assured that the school environment was not creating any undue anxiety for her. In fact, on the two days she initially attended, she settled into her new classroom and peer group very well.

I then met with the parents, presenting as very distraught, despairing, and wornout—like old "dish towels." They looked utterly frustrated and confused at not knowing what was happening to their daughter nor how to get her to come and stay in school. The parents confessed that their daughter went for a few weeks to pre-kindergarten and then refused to go. After a long struggle, they gave up and she won. They were afraid the same situation was reoccurring, and the same predictable outcome as well. But this could not be . . . the father-daughter relationship was always quite close and warm; however, now it had deteriorated as he expressed his anger at her, which included physical proportions. He had to drag her out of bed, put her in the shower and, physically, the parents dressed her.

My Recommendations

I felt compassion for this family. Repeated failures in trying to satisfy the school's expectation of regular attendance left the girl and her parents in a state of crisis; everyone seemed totally stressed. I decided to relieve them of the pressure and told the parents to go home and tell their daughter that she would not have to go back to school "for a while." I decided that it would be a gradual process where we would all support her success in returning to school, step by step. I told the parents they need not worry about the school's expectation; I would speak with the principal. I intended to reframe the "problem" of school "refusal" to a necessary and normal human need of grieving over her losses in the relocation process. (The family had recently moved to this area.)

Encouraging the Family to Be an Instrument of Change

With the goal of rekindling the love and joy in the parent-child relationships, I strongly encouraged the parents to do the following:

- Relax, go home, and share your perceptions of your daughter's strengths and wonderful qualities as you hug her.

- Share your dreams of her potential and present capabilities.

- Review her past successes and share some of your dreams. (The intent here was to create positive images, feelings and goals, restoring a strong family unit that had been destroyed.)

- Express your confidence in your daughter's intelligence and problem-solving abilities in meeting the current challenge of defeating whatever is blocking her from returning to school. Be mindful that she was able to return to kindergarten in a past successful event that she mastered.

- Use your current problem-solving skills that you are using now in building your own new business at home. Share your joy in successful accomplishments in your step-by-step process.

- Arrange for a complete physical examination by a pediatrician in order to rule out any medical problems and sexual abuse. I told them that our first family session would begin after I had the results.

The Treatment Process

After creating the relationship and "joining" with the parents, I reframed "the problem" as something all of them as a family needed to own and address—that being a *normal* life problem of adjusting to change. Relocating in a new city was difficult for the whole family. Their daughter needed time to adapt to new life circumstances *after* she did some grief work and healed enough to let go of the past. The parents agreed that a good new beginning can only follow a good ending and the whole family needed to bring their experiences and attachments from their past familiar world (neighborhood, house, pets, friends, school) to an appropriate and comfortable closure. Only then would their daughter be free to grab on to the new experiences that await her at her new school. The parents liked the idea of taking the focus off and making it a family project, to have everyone happy and successful in changing.

At the very beginning of our times together, I thanked the girl for her refusal to go to school! It had brought much needed attention to her needs and the family's needs to slow down and say good-bye completely to all their past experiences. We then proceeded to explore the losses associated in moving to a new city and the resulting painful feelings, normalizing them. We explored the process of change, recalling the dinosaurs, the weather, and our physical bodies. I praised her parents and father in particular (since their relationship was suffering the most) for their love and courage in leaving a secure home and moving to a new city. Using the *Lion King* metaphor that she liked, I explained that her father was brave like a *lion,* taking the risk to make a change because he wanted to be with his family much more than he could in his past job. Her father opened the door to a bright, promising future that she could help create. We used a video to explore these ideas. Everyone participated, sharing their own losses, fears, and sadness.

We then began to focus on her future attendance at school again. She stated she could return on Monday; however, I encouraged her to go slow, no need to rush. (I did this so that if she reneged on the promise, she would not be embarrassed.) We *externalized* the problem as sadness.

LF: "Someday, when sadness and anxiousness about new changes are not bothering or controlling you so much as now, what will you be doing differently or more of?"

Then, we explored:

- How big is the sadness?
- What keeps the sadness around?
- When is it that you don't feel the influence of sadness?
- When is sadness not controlling you?

How do you think you might fight back and shrink its size?

In sessions thereafter, we brought out more and more of her past successes and competencies. She became more in contact with her strengths and we highlighted her confidence and competence in solving problems. One homework task involved using her vivid imagination in:

    a. creating a future picture of happiness at school

    b. creating a list of her needs in order to be prepared for school in the morning

    c. imagining she was going to school and needing to plan for whatever she needs at school

After three weeks, the principal stated that time was running out and that she might have to go on home correspondence for the rest of the year unless she returned to school very soon.

With the parents, we set up some target goals and broke them down into little steps, the idea being that of building on small successes and proceeding at a comfortable pace for everyone. The parents suggested to my query of what would be helpful, that their daughter would *first have to get out of bed and get dressed for school*. Then she would cooperate in getting into the truck and getting out of the truck in the school parking lot. Next, their daughter would actually go into the school and then walk into her classroom. We knew that once she was in class, she would be fine.

On the designated week we planned, I phoned from my house at breakfast time to check and support the parents in the process. Their daughter refused to get out of bed. I asked to speak to her from under the bed covers where she was hiding. Under the safe and dark confines of her blankets, the telephone was accepted by her and we engaged in a wonderful fifteen-minute conversation. We spoke of the weekend visit from her favorite friend and talked about some of the exciting things they did together.

Eventually, I asked her to crawl out from under the covers and go to the window and give me a weather report. Without hesitation, she did so. I requested that she choose her clothes as if she were to go to school, stating that if she wanted to, all she was expected to do was just get into the parking lot. This was the only expectation to ensure success and build on this cooperation and trust. The next day she got dressed and came right into the school but refused to stay. I thanked her for coming in, praised her for her ability to defeat the *feeling monster*, which we had externalized.

I invited her teacher to meet us outside in the hallway and speak with her. However, at the suggestion to enter the class, she refused and wanted to go home, claiming nausea was influencing her. I was assured by her mother that physically she was fine. I noticed that her mother appeared to have some part in this "dance" so I took her aside and my suspicions were confirmed. Mother agreed that her daughter had a charming and powerful way to melt her firmness, i.e., *"the way she looks at me. . ."*

It was agreed to let the father handle the situation while the mother sat in the truck. While the teacher and the father stayed with the daughter, I walked the mother to the truck. She was shocked when I recommended that she lock her doors and not allow her daughter to come into the truck at recess time. Meanwhile, the teacher and her father persuaded the girl to walk into the classroom. The girl's only request was that her father be there at all times. Agreed! He stayed with her the entire day, taking only periodic walks to the library, water fountain, washroom, etc. His daughter shared that she was happy about her day and was excited about returning to school the next day. The next day her father could not stay at school and she claimed to be "sick" for the rest of the week. We took this as a sign to slow down and resumed the following week.

Again, she had difficulty staying so the principal and I helped to calm her down and assured her of our care and support along with her need to stay in school and her parents' need to go to work. She quickly relaxed. After apparently "throwing up" in the washroom, she needed lots of persistent reassurance that we would take care of her and she didn't need to go home yet. I asked if she would like to step outside for a breath of fresh air and, in doing so, she spied her parents returning with her lunch. They waved at each other yet the girl didn't run after them! She felt better and it helped her to settle into the classroom.

Getting Settled

I stayed with her, observing her ability to quickly engage in classroom routines and be accepted by classmates. At lunch, she appeared happy and told me I could leave and she would be fine now. Then she went off with her friends.

I spent every morning that week with her. She was able to kiss her parents good-bye and come into school on her own by week's end. By the next week, she was getting over the "morning sickness" that prevented her from eating breakfast. After two more weeks of daily support, I was able to wean my support to a couple of mornings. By this time Christmas was arriving and she met me with her mother at my central office with a Christmas present—she made a beautiful box filled with chocolate macaroons, which she baked especially for me. The parents added a huge bottle of ruby red wine in thanksgiving. We spoke and exchanged hugs, followed by a Christmas card the next day at school. After the holidays, she was fine, eager and ready to get back to school.

My guess is that this young girl suffered a number of losses and slipped temporarily back to an earlier place in her childhood for her needs to be met and to gain security. She is presently very happy as are her parents, teacher, principal . . . and me.

"The solution-focused approach directs us to meet needs,

not to force change in response to our needs. . ."

—*Larry Furmanczyk, 1996*

"Helping Parents and Children to Externalize Their Problems . . . at the Same Time" —Karen Rayter, Counselor and Consultant, Winnipeg, Manitoba

The Case

In working with parents in the school system as well as in private practice, I spend much of my time teaching and modeling for parents how to interact with their children in a way that is reassuring for their child as well as confidence-building for the parent. Parents often are so overwhelmed by their own feelings of fear and inadequacy in their parenting, they will render themselves helpless and powerless as their confidence continues on a downhill slide. I see one of my major tasks as helping parents regain a sense of personal power as parents:

- to be able to communicate with their child in a positive way
- to be able to clearly establish some boundaries
- to be able to make decisions and follow through no matter what situation comes their way

Sarah's mother, Judy, was referred to me by a school counselor who had attended one of my training workshops in Solution-Focused Brief Therapy. In our initial conversation on the telephone, she said that her third grade daughter needed help: Sarah was acting out at school; fighting with her classmates; coming home miserable; throwing massive temper tantrums at home; and generally wreaking havoc on the entire family. She continued to say that Sarah was threatening to run away; was constantly complaining of being "too fat"; and had lately been saying that she should just "kill herself." Judy's fears were that something was terribly wrong with Sarah, that she was either terribly depressed and suicidal, as well as on her way to an eating disorder. Mom's overwhelming feelings of "fear" and "helplessness" were rendering her to tears daily. She felt completely inadequate in managing Sarah's outbursts, and became emotionally distraught when Sarah began to talk of suicide.

The First Visit

I met with mom and Sarah together, Sarah with her toy stuffed lamb in her arms. She was very talkative and outgoing, easily talking about all the extracurricular activities in which she participated.

In asking what her understanding was of why she was here, Sarah said she was getting into too much trouble at school and that she was a "dummy." She was fighting with her friends and spending a lot of time in the hall for a "time out." Exploring this further, she described many of her fights as competing with friends as to "Who gets to play the 'Nanny" (from the television show), which her friends played every day during free time. She said she always wanted to play the star of the show, and really got very angry when her friends wanted their turn.

Her typical style was to become verbally aggressive, hurting her friends' feelings, take her anger out on other kids in the class (one boy in particular who was very shy and insecure would often get a cuff across the back of the head). Her anger would then turn to sadness when her friends in turn would no longer play with her and exclude her from other activities during the day. Sarah continued to give examples of situations that were happening at school. She did not bring up anything about what was happening at home, so I did not pursue that at the time.

Mom added some perceptions at this point, saying that Sarah was coming home very mad every day from school, not listening to her parents, talking back, and not cooperating at all. She wisely did not bring up her more serious concerns with Sarah present. Things generally escalated to the point that there would be a verbal confrontation, with Sarah not backing down from the challenge. Her mother chuckled as she described her daughter as "very assertive," although at this point I was reading tremendous resignation on her face. I knew that Mom had a lot more to say!

Sarah agreed with her mother's concern of how angry and upset Sarah seemed to be lately, sheepishly grinning and cuddling into mom. I asked Sarah to give me an idea of what she was feeling when she was angry.

Sarah: "I don't know, it's like I'm having a good time and then something happens and I get mad, and I just can't stop getting madder and madder. . . . It's like I get really grouchy and then I'm grouchy at everybody."

I asked Sarah if she could *predict* when the "grouchies" were going to happen, when they were coming. Sarah responded by saying she did not know when it was going to happen.

Sarah: "They just come from somewhere and take over . . . and when that happens they just ruin my whole day."

I asked Sarah if she had ever been able to stop these *grouchies* once they began to ruin her day. She shook her head "No," and said she didn't think there was anything she could do to stop them.

After asking Sarah if she would like to stop them, she nodded "Yes" vigorously. I asked her if she would like to try a little experiment for the next week. I went over to my stuffed animals that she had been eyeing throughout the meeting, and brought out "Oscar the Grouch." (What child wouldn't recall Oscar from *Sesame Street*?) I sat the stuffed toy on the coffee table by us and asked Sarah if she knew who he was. She enthusiastically replied "Oscar the Grouch," and then looked at me as if I was from another planet and thinking "Who wouldn't know who he was?"

KR: Let's say Oscar is having a very grouchy day and decides that he really wants to ruin your day too. He has the grouchies and he is coming to bring them to you. Is there anything you would like to say to him, Sarah?"

Mom, who was watching all of this with a look of bewilderment on her face, then saw her daughter stand up assertively with hands firmly planted on her hips.

Sarah: "There sure is! Mr. Grouch . . . I'm tired of you . . . you are making me feel bad when you ruin my day. I don't want you around when you are like this . . . so you can just go away! You can only come near me again when you are happy . . . .and I mean it!!"

I asked Sarah if she thought she could say this when she felt the grouchies coming on. She assured me that she could. I asked her how she was going to know when they were coming. She again reassured me that she would know from now on. At this point, we agreed that she would keep track of the times during school when she was able to tell "the grouchies" to go away and leave her alone. She was very excited at the very thought of trying this. I then asked Sarah if she would play in the waiting room for a few minutes while I spoke to her mom. She skipped out of the room with her toy lamb in tow.

Mom sat quietly for a few minutes, as if digesting what she had witnessed with her daughter. She was not sure if the session was "serious enough," given the possibility that something might be seriously wrong with Sarah. I acknowledged Mom's view that Sarah was indeed a powerful child with tremendous resources (normalizing the problem), and cooperated with her feeling that parenting her might result in having to be one step ahead of her all of the time.

We set up a follow-up appointment for two weeks. I asked Mom to notice any of the times during the next two weeks when Sarah was managing her "grouchies" any differently, and to acknowledge it to Sarah. Mom thought that maybe saying anything to Sarah might set her off, so she said that maybe she had just better notice the differences to herself. She left my office very skeptically and joined Sarah (who was busy ripping perfume samples out of all my magazines and declaring that she was going to become a vegetarian). Mom smilingly rolled her eyes as if to say "See what I mean?" And they left.

Second Visit

Sarah and mom came to the second visit with Mom noticeably smiling more. I had Oscar on the table and Sarah noticed immediately. I asked: "What's better?" and I heard "A lot is better!" I asked Sarah to describe them in detail. Again, Sarah stood up with her hands on her hips and demonstrated how she managed her meetings with Mr. Grouch.

She had only been sent for one time-out during the two weeks. She was allowing her friend to play the "Nanny," although reluctantly. Even the boy who got a regular cuff on the head was spared from her "grouchies." We explored what differences this new behavior was making.

I asked Mom what she noticed that was different. She shyly admitted to me how skeptical she was when she left, and that she couldn't believe what a difference she saw in Sarah. She also discussed her own anxieties and how her own catastrophizing was really getting in the way of her parenting. Mom was *externalizing* her own problems! She agreed that she really needed to restore her personal power as a parent.

Mom blushingly admitted that over the last two weeks that she was helping Sarah talk to Mr. Grouch (feeling like a fool, and all of the time repeating the words I had used with Sarah). She said this had been very helpful for her to do.

> *Indeed, Mom was beginning to externalize her "grouchies" along with her daughter's.*

Although Mom was bringing her daughter in for me to focus on, I couldn't help but feel that Mom was going through some of the same changes as Sarah. She was gaining confidence in her parenting; was beginning to feel that a lot of her feelings were normal; and. most important, was learning how to talk to her daughter in a way that demonstrated that they both had some control over the problem.

During my third and last visit with them, Mom told me she had now met with some other mothers of kids in Sarah's class. Previously she had withdrawn from other parents; she had feelings that they were also noticing how "out of control" her daughter was. This had led her to isolate herself from others because of her own insecurities. She was now beginning to find out that these mothers were having very similar problems to hers (she was normalizing herself now). She also got Sarah's teacher on track (without any prompting from me), and asked *her* to notice any time that Sarah was sharing the "Nanny" role or any other cooperative gesture, and asked her to compliment Sarah on her efforts.

Mom also told me that she was no longer frightened "for" or "of" her daughter. She looked different to me during this last visit; she had that quiet confidence that strong parenting reflects, and her interactions with Sarah were much more spontaneous and less cautious and calculated. She left saying she wanted to make a follow-up appointment, but I have yet to hear from her.

"Truth is such a rare thing, it is a delight to tell it."

—*Emily Dickinson*

Dear Parents,

The stories described here all have several things in common; they describe; courageous parents who chose to *never give up on their kids;* children and adolescents who listened to their families when they *felt important* to them; competencies and strengths of family members and troubled kids that *triumphed* over problems; love and responsibility that created an environment in which children and adolescents were *less influenced* by pressures in the world today.

I hope this book relays a strong message to you ... that you indeed have the abilities to assist your kids to be their best. Your job is to find them. The quote below may share the possibility of the future as you discover the solutions within yourself:

"Never put off until tomorrow what you can do today, because if you enjoy it today, you can do it again tomorrow."

—*Anonymous*

Best Wishes,

Linda Metcalf

References

American Psychiatric Association. (1995). *Diagnostic and Statistical Manual of Mental Disorders, IIIR.* Washington, D.C.: American Psychiatric Association.

Agel, J., and Glanze, Walter. (1987). *Pearls of Wisdom: A Harvest of Quotations From All Ages.* New York: Harper & Row Publishers.

Cade, Barry. (1995). *Behaviour and Discipline—Policy or Practice?* Wolverhampton, England. (At Press).

Cade, Brian. (1995). *Discipline: Insolence, Offensiveness and Violence.* Sydney, Australia. (At Press).

Cade, Brian. (1994). "Treating the House Like a Hotel." *Case Studies in Brief and Family Therapy,* 8 (1): 5-14.

Cade, Brian, and O'Hanlon, W. (1993). *A Brief Guide to Brief Therapy.* New York: W.W. Norton.

Covey, S. (1990). *The Seven Habits of Highly Effective People: Powerful Lessons in Personal Change.* New York: Fireside Books, a Division of Simon & Schuster.

De Shazer, S. (1985). *Keys to Solutions in Brief Therapy.* New York: W.W. Norton.

Durrant, M. (1995). *Creative Strategies for School Problems.* New York: W.W. Norton.

Epston, D. (1989). *Collected Papers.* Adelaide, South Australia: Dulwich Centre Publications.

Epston, D., and White, M. (1990). *Narrative Means to Therapeutic Ends.* New York: W.W. Norton.

Fulghum, R. (1989). *It Was on Fire When I Lay Down on It.* New York: Random House.

Fulghum, R. (1995). *From Beginning to End: The Rituals of Our Lives.* New York: Villard Books.

Kuehl, B. (1995). "The Solution-Oriented Genogram: A Collaborative Approach." *Journal of Marital and Family Therapy,* Vol. 21, 3, 239–249.

McGoldrick, M., and Gerson, R. (1985). *Genograms in Family Assessment.* New York: W.W. Norton.

Metcalf, L. (1995). *Counseling Toward Solutions: A Practical Solution-Focused Program for Working with Students, Teachers, and Parents.* New York: Center for Applied Research in Education.

Metcalf, L. (1995). "Great Expectations: How Changing Your Thinking Can Change Your Students." *Learning Magazine,* March, 1995, 93–95.

Miller, W. (1985). "Motivation for Treatment: A Review with Special Emphasis on Alcoholism." *Psychological Bulletin,* 98 (1), 84–107.

Moore, T. (1992). *Care of the Soul: A Guide for Cultivating Depth and Sacredness in Everyday Life.* New York: HarperCollins.

Myerhoff, B. (1986). "Life Not Death in Venice; Its Second Life," in Turner, V.W. and Bruner, E.M. (eds.), *The Anthropology of Experience.* Chicago: University of Illinois Press.

Morgan, Marlo. (1994). *Mutant Message Down Under.* New York: HarperCollins.

O'Hanlon, W.H., and Weiner-Davis, M. (1989). *In Search of Solutions.* New York: W.W. Norton.

O'Hanlon, W.H. (1994). Informational Sheets from *Possibilities.* (Omaha: The Hudson Center for Brief Therapy.)

Redfield, J. (1993). *The Celestine Prophecy: An Adventure.* New York: Warner Books.

Santrock, J. (1994). *Child Development.* Iowa: Brown and Benchmark.

Watzlawick, P., Weakland, J., and Fisch, R. (1974). *Change: Principles of Problem Formation and Problem Resolution.* New York: W.W. Norton

Weiner-Davis, M. (1992). *Divorce Busting: A Revolutionary and Rapid Program for Staying Together.* New York: Simon & Schuster.

White, M. (1989). "Saying Hullo Again: The Incorporation of the Lost Relationship in the Resolution of Grief." *Selected Papers.* Adelaide, South Australia: Dulwich Centre Publications.

Woolfolk, A. (1995). *Educational Psychology.* Boston: Allyn & Bacon.

Index